Digital Sex Work

How Your Webcam, Cell Phone & Pedicure Can Make You Rich

By RedPedSole

Copyright 2014 by RedPedSole
Published by RedPedSole

This ebook is licensed for your personal enjoyment only. This ebook may not be re-sold or given away to other people. If you would like to share this book with another person, please purchase an additional copy for each recipient. If you're reading this book and did not purchase it, or it was not purchased for your enjoyment only, then please return to Smashwords.com or your favorite retailer and purchase your own copy. Thank you for respecting the hard work of this author.

BONUS CONTENT

Thank you for downloading this e-book. Even before you read this book, I would like to say "Thank You!" in a very meaningful way. Please fill out your e-mail address to receive our

8-Day eCourse, Newsletter and Updates[1]

TABLE OF CONTENTS

BONUS CONTENT 2
PREFACE 5
   Sex Work 5
   Are You Born To Be Worshiped? 5
   The Many Benefits of Launching Your Own Amateur Foot Fetish Empire: 6
   What You Will Learn In This Book: 6
   Why You Should Read This Book 8
INTRODUCTION 1
   50 Shades of Foot Fetish and Mommy Porn 1
   Goddess Worship: Why Men Are Obsessed With Women's Feet 1
   Criminally Obsessed With Feet 2
   Is Foot Fetish A Sexual Perversion? 3
   Remembering Rex Ryan 4
   Quentin Tarantino's Foot Fetish Obsession 4
   Be A Responsible Adult 5
   Why Foot Fetish Is Becoming So Popular 6
   Defining A Foot Fetish 7
CHAPTER 1 11
   How To Become An Amateur Foot Goddess Model 11
   Developing Your Foot Fetish Theme 12
   Ethnic Foot Fetishes: What Is The Obsession With Asian Feet? 14
   Indian Feet & The Beauty of Indian Henna Foot Designs 14
   Softcore vs. Hardcore 16
   Feet with Face or Just Feet? 16
   Choose Your Online Publishing Platform(s) 17
   Setting Up Your Wordpress Foot Fetish Blog 18
   The Free Site vs. Fee Site 18
   Tease With Free To Get Your Fee! 19

CHAPTER 2 20
Best Types of Pics, Vids and Shoes 20
PICS 20
Flipinista: A Woman's BFF "Best Flip Flop" 22
Who Is Monique Friedman? 23
The Many Grand Things about Flipinista 23
Invest in a Good Fashion Statement 23
Foot Fetish Pics & Vids Examples: 24
Your Most Controversial or Suggestive Foot Photo Shoot 25
Your First Foot Fetish Video: 26
You Bring me JOI or JOE: 26
The Sound of Soles Slapping 27

CHAPTER 3 29
Your At Home Personal Studio 29
To Light or Not To Light 29
Frequency: How Often Should You Produce New Content? ... 30

CHAPTER 4 31
Foot Fetish Money Makers 31

CHAPTER 5 57
Promoting Your Foot Fetish Empire 57
Find, Create and Build Your Foot Fetish Community 57

CHAPTER 6 67
Interviews with Four Amateur Foot Fetish Models 67

RESOURCES & RECOMMENDATIONS 92
ABOUT THE AUTHOR 93
ACKNOWLEDGMENTS 94
Index 95

PREFACE

Sex Work[2]

Wikipedia defines it as; *"the exchange of sexual services, performances, or products for material compensation. It includes activities of direct physical contact between buyers and sellers... as well as indirect sexual stimulation".* But what if it is in digital form? What if it's merely taking pictures or video of your feet and posting it on the web for men and women to do whatever they do when watching feet? Is it sex work then?

In this book, Digital Sex Work: How Your Webcam, Cell Phone & Pedicure Can Make You Rich, you will learn how to secretly and covertly earn passive income from taking pics & vids of your feet and posting them online without having to launch a website!

However, before we get started in showing you how to make money with your web cam and camera phone using your feet, I want to be very clear that the author of this book in no way, shape or form is promoting any type of prostitution. This book is recommended for women age 18+ and not intended to be pornographic or degrading to women in any way.

This book is designed to be informative and educational for the millions of men and women who have a foot fetish and would like to discover how they can legitimately earn a living taking videos/photos of their feet. Digital Sex Work: How Your Webcam, Cell Phone & Pedicure Can Make You Rich is about celebrating a woman's full sexuality and self-empowerment. There is no age limit to launching your own foot fetish empire and there are many women online right now who are earning income and posting photos/videos of their gorgeous feet in their 80's and dare I say 90's such as the *Erotic Crone*[3] on Fetlife. So don't let age come between you and your toes! LOL

Are You Born To Be Worshiped?

If you found the title of this book and its contents interesting or intriguing, it probably means you were born to be worshiped, admired and exalted by men and women; if not from your head to your toes then in reverse! That being said, if you apply just a small portion of this action steps in this book, you are going to have to get used to being in charge of an enormous male fan base and owing your sexual domination!

This book is designed to turn you into an amateur foot fetish goddess, guru or star. There will be countless men (and women) who will literally worship the ground you walk on and make you feel like a million bucks just sharing your precious peds with them. And who knows, you might just make a million bucks following the suggestions in this book!

The Many Benefits of Launching Your Own Amateur Foot Fetish Empire:

- You can make money 24/7 on your own terms
- You don't have to worry about copyright infringement or licensing since you are taking pictures and videos of your own feet
- You can create as much or as little content as you want
- You can set your own hours
- You don't have to share your earnings, or publishing rights with a publishing house
- You know, love and believe in the product; your feet!
- You don't need a lot of (and in most cases zero) startup money
- You can truly do it yourself (DIY)
- You can be private, discreet and keep your anonymity or go public and become a foot goddess guru

What You Will Learn In This Book:

- I am going to show you How To Become An Amateur Foot Goddess Model by developing your Foot Fetish

Theme

- The different types of Foot Fetish and how to choose between softcore and hardcore
- How to Choose Your Online Publishing Platform(s)
- How to Up Your Wordpress Foot Fetish Blog
- How to take pictures/videos of your feet and post them online to make instant income
- You will discover Your Most Controversial or Suggestive Foot Photo Shoot
- How to choose the best types of photos/videos of your feet
- How pick the best blog/website platform
- You will learn how often you should produce content
- The best natural lighting arrangement
- How to use your camera phone and/or webcam to produce unlimited content
- How to launch your foot fetish empire without a website
- You will learn the top 18 platforms to launch your foot fetish empire
- Read one-on-one interviews with actual amateur foot fetish women who spill the beans on what works and what doesn't
- How to use social media to launch and promote your foot fetish business
- How to use micro outsourcing platforms to earn instant income with photos/videos of your feet
- How to use Amazon.com to acquire anything you want for free
- How to use the naughty side of Ebay to earn substantial profits with your tootsies
- Sixteen immediate and easy foot fetish money makers that don't require you to have a website
- Four Q&A interviews with successful amateur Foot Fetish Goddesses

Why You Should Read This Book

I had an epiphany or an "ah ha" moment when I realized that there are millions of women out there who could easily earn substantial income; earning discreet digital income using one of their best God-given assets, but have no idea how to go about it. So, I decided I might as well show others how easy it is to do.

Although, I'm an Internet Marketing Specialist, you don't have to be internet savvy to launch your own foot fetish empire, nor do you have to be a professional photographer or foot model. In fact, simply using the camera or video on your phone, there are millions of women around the world taking advantage of the amateur foot fetish market. It is booming just like reality TV, because people like seeing the real thing versus something scripted and highly stylized. Another reason the amateur foot fetish industry is soaring to new heights is because it has moved from mere internet voyeurism to economic consumerism. Women can now make money with their feet and never have to show their face if they choose not to.

Highly educated women are launching foot fetish sites, and providing digital sex work services to pay for college, stay-at-home moms are earning extra income and treating it as a home based business. Some women are paying their rent or the mortgage. Regardless of the reason, launching your own foot fetish site has never been more simple and need I say in today's economy; necessary!

In the Huffington Post, an article written by Dr. Yvonne K. Fulbright entitled, _"Is Sex Work Becoming 'No Big Deal'?"_[4], it says a British study, published in the journal, Sex Education, found that 16.5% of undergraduates would consider sex work, with 93% pointing to money as the primary incentive. Another Leeds University study, involving over 200 lap-dancers, reported that one in three participants engaged in such work to fund their schooling.

According to _Nouse, York_[5] students turn to sex work to fund degrees. Dozens of university students in York have turned to sex work as they struggle to fund their degrees, Nouse revealed. As many as 30 students in York are operating as escorts, and eight agencies in the area were able to provide student escorts. One agency said they had up to seven students available.

In an exclusive Q&A interview I found and excerpted from the *Philippe Matthews*[6] radio show with sex expert, Dr. Yvonne K. Fulbright, she spoke openly about the new reality of Sex Work:

Host:

I read in the Huffington Post that you wrote a book called Sex Work Becoming 'No Big Deal.' This is an old term that has a new twist it seems like, as the economy has taken a dip. Young people and older people have chosen to use technology in a completely different way. Can you talk about this a little bit?

Yvonne:

Sure. There was a University of Arkansas study that was put out that found that a number of U.S. women are actually going to work as far as high quality illegal prostitution and what was meant by that is that they were either going to the internet and advertising themselves or joining high end escort services.

Host:

That is amazing. This is, I guess, a new trend that basically you could do anonymously. What do you think the moral implications, if any, are?

Yvonne:

Well, this definitely depends on who you ask. The research also indicated that a number of these women are educated, a number of them reported coming from a strong family background. They weren't necessarily street kids or people from broken homes, but they were seeing this as a way to make money, provide more stability and autonomy. At the same time, some of them are also saying, "I'm getting some job satisfaction out of this," which is actually reflective of similar studies that have been done in Australia, where sex work is handled much more differently and more legally than it is over here. This all comes down to a person's value system and moral system, as far as if this is problematic or not.

For me, I feel that if a person is doing it from a place of empowerment and doing it safely and taking care of their sexual health and those of their clients first and foremost, then I would need to withhold any judgment I would have over those kinds of interactions, because ultimately at the end of the day, it's none of my business, if it's not doing any harm to anybody besides those two involved.

It appears that trading money for foot fun and foot fetish is more than doable! In fact, its not just women in the U.S., who have found financial efficacy online, Berlin Studies Centre study has reported that one in three university students in Berlin would consider sex work as a way to pay for their education. It further found that over 29% of university students in Paris and 18.5% in Kiev would contemplate such. Some 4% of the 3,200 Berlin participants reported already having engaged in some type of sex work, like erotic dancing, Internet performances, or prostitution. Researchers speculated that greater student workloads and higher fees have made sex work's high hourly wages quite attractive.

These "artistic performers," as they are often called, don't feel victimized. As Dr. Fulbright mentioned, some women cite perks of the job, like more money made in less time, a flexible work schedule, a sense of independence, and anonymity are all strong motivators.

Digital Sex Work:

INTRODUCTION

50 Shades of Foot Fetish and Mommy Porn

Mommy Porn; this is another one of the many labels that your online foot fetish empire will fall under. The term has gained tremendous popularity due to the book that took the world by storm and the movie that has since been made. 50 Shades of Grey sold more than 40 million copies all over the world in an extremely short amount of time and stayed on the best-seller's list of USA Today for more than 15 weeks—definitely a record!

According to an excerpt from the _Philippe Matthews Show blog_[7], it's expected that romance fiction such as this is going to attract millions of young adults, especially if they have very open minds about sex. Interestingly, they found that 50 Shades of Grey also appealed to another demographic: moms. This novel has created quite a buzz along with a new genre; "mommy porn", it has become a mainstream word and now women or moms with beautiful feet can be associated with it.

Psychologists have tried to explain to explain this new literary and societal genre by first recognizing that this type of book is easy to read, thus a perfect companion while mothers wait for their kids to finish school or while the washing machine does its job.

It also has something to do with the presence of a lot of platforms in which the book can be read. Tablets, dedicated e-book readers, and smart phones now allow these moms to carry mommy porn anywhere they go without detection or feeling embarrassed.

Goddess Worship: Why Men Are Obsessed With Women's Feet

I guess it's safe to say as the author of this book, I _worship women_[8]; their feet, their legs, and their EVERYTHING! Not to sound cliche, but to me, women are truly the greatest creation God could have ever made, which is why I love the joke that God must be a man because their is nothing on earth more beautiful than a well groomed, well pedicured woman!

Digital Sex Work:

Obsession as it is defined, is a compulsive preoccupation or fixation of an idea or a thing. In the case of this book, as to why men are obsessed with women's feet is only in the mind of the foot fetish. Whether there is an unusual interest in feet, foot accessories or footwear, men with this kind of obsession find gratification in touching, massaging, watching, licking, sucking or kissing a woman's feet. Studies show that this is a form of submission to women. Men would adore and kiss a women's feet just like a beautiful, mystical goddess being worshiped. Most women would love to be treated like this and if you look into the mind of a man staring and admiring a woman's nicely pedicured foot, it could connote that the man might also be sexually interested in the woman other than her feet. Her perfectly pedicured toes of course are connected to a nice pair of legs and we all know what they lead to…

Criminally Obsessed With Feet

However, your pretty little peds could get you into trouble when dealing with some men who are truly obsessed with women's feet such as a Jackson, Tennessee man with Foot Fetish charged with stalking as reported by _WATN-TV Local 24 News_[9], had a history of asking women to show him their feet and was arrested after trespassing into a woman's apartment to watch her sleep. In Sacramento, California, a _Homeless Man With Foot Fetish Plead No Contest To Charges_[10] and faced up to 6 years in prison for his obsession with women's feet according to Sacramento CBS 13.

William Russell, was accused of stalking women so he could suck on their toes and pleaded no contest to two counts of first-degree burglary, one count of sexual battery and one count of attempted sexual battery under a plea agreement, the Sacramento County District Attorney's office announced. He will be sentenced to 6 years and 10 months in prison and will be required to register as a sex offender when he's released on parole.

In the exclusive CBS 13 jailhouse interview, Russell declared his criminal weakness for exposed toes. _"I've had a fetish all my life and it's always been under control and stuff,"_ he said. _"I'd massage them at least, or suck them. I remember I was younger sucking_ toes." He admitted that his obsession, and love for women's toes put him behind bars. *"God allowed me to love feet, female feet."*

Is Foot Fetish A Sexual Perversion?

As a result of this one man's conviction and foot obsession, the Sacramento prosecutor deemed foot fetish a 'sexual perversion' as reported in the [Sacramento News & Review](#)[11]. Click [here](#)[12] to read the official release from the district attorney's office.

CASE OF INTEREST

DATE: October 15, 2013
CASE: William Russell
PROSECUTOR: Deputy District Attorney Allison Dunham, Adult Sexual Assault

Prosecution

District Attorney Jan Scully announced today that William Russell pled no contest to two counts of first degree burglary, one count of sexual battery and one count of attempted sexual battery. The burglary offenses are strikes under California law.

Russell, who did not know the victims, took interest in the victims' toes and feet. He complimented both victims on their feet and asked if he could touch them. Both victims declined and tried to ignore him. Russell then followed both victims to their apartments and forced his way inside. He sexually assaulted one victim and tried to sexually assault the other victim, but she was able to push him out of her apartment.

Deputy District Attorney Allison Dunham states, "The defendant's sexual perversion led to acts of violence that terrified these innocent women. He will now face significant consequences for these crimes and will have to register as a convicted sex offender for the rest of his life."

Under the plea agreement, Russell will be sentenced to a stipulated 6 years and 10 months in prison. Once he is released on parole, he will be required to register as a convicted sex offender. Sentencing

Digital Sex Work:

is scheduled for November 12, 2013 at 8:30 a.m. in Department 61 of the Sacramento Superior Court.

Remembering Rex Ryan

Of course, you could not talk about foot fetish obsession without brining up NLF star, Rex Ryan and his videos that [TMZ][13] blasted with the headline, "Jets Coach is 'Tarantino of Tootsies'!" They reported that the New York Jets head coach's fancy footwork made him a star as he was offered a trip to Vegas and his very own foot fetish booth at the [Adult Entertainment Expo][14].

TMZ further reported that CLIPS4SALE.com, which boasts the biggest fetish clip store online, extended a $10,000 offer for Ryan and his wife Michelle to sign autographs and take pictures in their very own booth at the porn convention.

It all stems from a report on Deadspin.com, which claimed to have unearthed foot fetish videos starring Michelle Ryan, and filmed by Rex, which had been posted online under the user name "ihaveprettyfeet." CLIPS4SALE was so impressed with Rex's directing skills -- they coined him the "Tarantino of Tootsies," and believe Michelle and her "heavenly hooves" could be the biggest seller on their site. They've even offered to change the booth colors to green and white in honor of the Jets.

Here is another [Rex Ryan Foot Video][15] that swept the internet. An offer has been sent over to the Jets camp -- but no word on whether Ryan's ready to put his best foot forward.

Quentin Tarantino's Foot Fetish Obsession

Speaking of Tarantino of Tootsies, its been long rumored that the A list producer/director has a foot fetish or at least cinematically. Uma Thurman toasted Quentin Tarantino's foot fetish by pouring and drinking champagne from her [Christian Louboutins][16]. Then there is the email and photos called, [The Quentin Tarantino Toe-Sucking Sex Email That Will Haunt Your Dreams][17] that will never go away.

According to a blog post called, "[Quentin Tarantino Talks Feet, Fear & Films][18]," by United Kingdom's Little White Lies, "Feet are

Digital Sex Work:

dangerous, sexy things in Tarantino's world. Bridget Fonda's ringed piggies seduce a killer in Jackie Brown. Thurman's paralyzed toes become screen-filling to(e)tems in Kill Bill. Kurt Russell gives Rosario Dawson's feet a tongue 'n' tickle in Death Proof. Christoph Waltz ominously undresses Diane Kruger's in Inglourious Basterds. And there's QT himself, using a vampy Salma Hayek's feet like a tequila flume in From Dusk Till Dawn."

There's even a gag Facebook page called *Quinton Tarantino's Foot Fetish*[19]. Someone took the time to find rare footage of Tarantino in a scene talking about feet with a collage of feet scenes from his movies in *Quentin Tarantino's Foot Fetish*[20]. But most will find it hilarious to watch this *Quentin Tarantino Spoof Compilation and Foot Scenes on YouTube.*[21]

Be A Responsible Adult

Another level of foot fetish obsession that crosses the line is when young, teenage girls who are starving for attention think foot fetish is a fun game and get caught up with perverts and predators from their lack of judgment along with their struggle for sexual identity and womanhood. In a disturbing excerpt titled, 'Lakeside Lolita', Hannah Anderson flirts with fetish on *Ask.fm*[22] in All Voices, they say "It has already been reported that Hannah Anderson "came unglued" on her Ask.fm profile this week, but the content of the Q&A is what inspires worry. Hannah is only 16-years-old, a teenage girl who has just gone through an extremely high profile incident that has many believing she is the victim of kidnapping. That is why it is just shocking that no responsible adult in her life is keeping an eye on her online behavior, especially since she is now sexually exploiting herself to anonymous perverts.

On her Ask.fm account Hannah acknowledges that the "weirdest" question she ever got was from an anonymous person who asked if he could "*suck her toes and massage her feet forever.*" However, she immediately began participating in a conversation about her feet with an anonymous poster who took interest in her, her dancing, and -- oddly -- her feet and what shoes she wore. This anonymous poster then requested that Hannah show a photo of her feet, to which she obliged happily, though she spoke of not liking feet in a playful manner.

Hannah Anderson may be unwittingly exploiting herself sexually to anonymous men (and perhaps women) who are getting off on her feet -- as she even admitted that those were the types of questions she was getting. It's hard to say if she is doing this on purpose. She couldn't possibly realize that these people are actually sexually exploiting her, but the details of her story are already stranger than fiction -- stranger than the Stanley Kubrick classic "Lolita."

Hannah's father, or someone in her life, needs to sit her down and explain to her what's going on with these fetish lovers who are sending her inappropriate comments about her feet. Perhaps she doesn't realize that this is a sexual fetish, but maybe she does. Regardless of her knowledge or involvement in this, this is still a 16-year-old girl and her openness on social media is leading her to sexually exploiting herself, right under the noses of all around her. She is already the talk of the town, so-to-speak, with plenty of rumors and speculation that she was sexually involved with Jim DiMaggio, so these foot fetish posts aren't helping her image any.

Why Foot Fetish Is Becoming So Popular

The answer is "I don't know". Fetish is a rapidly expanding minority. The statistics are not clear; yet, there is an increasing number of people who are "searching" for the meaning of this sexual fascination. This increasing minority may be the people who are born with a proclivity for this kind of sexual bias for female feet or others who might just be curious. Did you know the legendary "Elvis" had a foot fetish? Jay Leno has also admitted to having a great appreciation for women's feet and Tommy Lee is also a famous foot admirer.

There are countless hypotheses as to why foot fetishism is becoming more popular and mainstream. In an excerpt from a blog entry entitled, "_Celebrity Foot Fetish_[23]" by Wes Laurie as to why foot fetishism is becoming so popular, he says, "*The short answer: no one can truly say. One of the most popular theories is that the feet and the genitals occupy adjacent areas of the somatosensory cortex,*

Digital Sex Work:

possibly entailing some neural communication between the two. The mentioned cortex is a structure in the parietal lobe of the brain dealing with sensory input. Other theories abound, but once again formula variations make pinpointing the actual root cause on a whole scale impossible."

Foot Fetish is becoming so mainstream that on the Arsenio Hall Show, Michelle Trachtenberg talked about her foot fetish followers. Michelle Trachtenberg is an accomplished actor and an amazing person, but some people can't see past her feet. Michelle tells Arsenio what that's like. (Source: *IMDb*[24])

Defining A Foot Fetish

According to Wikipedia, *Foot fetishism*[25], foot partialism, foot worship, or podophilia is a pronounced sexual interest in feet. It is the most common form of sexual preference for otherwise non-sexual objects or body parts. Foot fetish has been defined as a pronounced sexual interest in the feet or footwear.

Freud considered foot binding as a form of fetishism. For a foot fetishist, points of attraction include the shape and size of the foot and toes (i.e., long toes, short toes, pointed toes, high arches, slender soles, fat toes, long toenails, short toenails, small feet, toenail color), jewelry, toe rings, ankle bracelets, treatments e.g.: french pedicure, state of dress (i.e., barefoot, flip flops, or clad in socks or nylons), odor, and any form of sensory interaction, e.g. licking, sucking, tickling, people giving foot jobs, pedal pumping and trampling/stomping.

In another excerpt from the Philippe Matthews Show with Dr. Yvonne K. Fulbright, when asked why is foot fetishism becoming so popular and what is the origin of the word fetish? Dr. Fulbright responded to the Q&A with…

> Yvonne:
>
> Actually, fetish the word is one of the most misunderstood words in sexual attraction when it comes to understanding sexual behaviors, with the foot fetish being a classic example of this. For somebody to have a foot fetish, for example, it's not an

actual fetish, but it's a case of what's called partialism, the partialism being a situation where a person has exclusive attraction to a body part. A fetish is a situation where a person has learned to attach a sexual significance to an object or to a behavior, which is in large part not considered erotic in nature. The most common fetishes tend to be objects like shoes, lingerie, things made of rubber or leather. I can talk more about the foot fetish in particular, if you'd like.

Philippe:
Sure.

Yvonne:

It's really a misnomer, if anything.

Philippe:
A misnomer how?

Yvonne:

Partialism is the situation specifically where a person has exclusive attraction to a body part, but the word fetish originally had nothing to do with sex and it was actually derived from the Portuguese word feitico and I don't know if I'm saying it correctly, because I don't speak Portuguese, but old world Portuguese explorers used that term to describe any religious artifacts regarded by tribal cultures as having magical powers. Then, it was in the 19th century that fetish started to be used to describe some things that sexually excites a person.

Philippe:
Okay. Moving forward, how would we categorize this attraction to feet, because most people say foot fetish, but foot impartialism doesn't sound as sexy.

Yvonne:

No.

Digital Sex Work:

Philippe:
Hey, he has foot impartialism, he's impartial to feet. What would be an appropriate term in conversation to use about this particular type of concept of sexual attraction?

Yvonne:

I think the word attraction pretty much captures it or eroticism or even fascination, because it's not even just the foot as a possible sexual object, but it's that people like the touch of the foot or the odor of the foot. I've known dominatrices where their client will come in, ask her to put on a pair of sneakers and go for a jog before getting busy, because all he wants to do is smell her feet or smell the shoes, because that's the most sexually enticing part of the whole social sexual interaction.

Philippe:
Fascinating. I'm just going to use it as a general term here on this interview for time reasons, so would foot fetish be considered under the BDSM category or the kink category or where does that fit in all of this new resurgence of taboo sex.

Yvonne:

Where would a foot fetish fit into that whole picture?

Philippe:
Yes.

Yvonne:

Quite honestly, I think it depends on who you ask, because we don't know why people develop a fetish, how it develops, and it can be looked at as healthy obsessive fascination or enthusiasm and then you could equate it to somebody getting really enthusiastic about collecting baseball cards. That's a pastime that's considered really harmless, so why should obsessing over feet be any weirder, kinkier, more "abnormal" than somebody fetishizing, if you want to say that, over baseball cards and baseball players? You can cast it as something sexual or you could say it's something more of a pastime or even just a natural part of human development for some people, this fixation on the feet. Honestly, at the end of the day, most of these fetishes are harmless and if anything, they're something that could be envied because you always have something there that turns you on, an arousal object or behavior, so there's something to envy about it in that way.

I think because so many people feel judged for having this kind of attraction, no matter what it is, it tends to get cast in the unusual or kink behavior category.

Philippe:
Sure.

Yvonne:

Honestly, there's not enough research on these things to know how many people are into it or not. I would venture to guess that there are more people with some type of "fetish" than what we realize.

Listen to the entire interview with Dr. Yvonne K. Fulbright from the link below:

More from Dr. Yvonne K. Fulbright:

Official Website[26]
Twitter[27]

Digital Sex Work:

CHAPTER 1

How To Become An Amateur Foot Goddess Model

To showcase oneself in front of the camera involves some degree of guts and passion. They say, successful models need not be overly beautiful, they only need to "make love to the camera". True enough, many women have found a niche in the modeling industry, despite the flaws that they think they have. Foot fetish models must be able to start modeling their feet first in their minds. Like any other task, modeling, involves a great deal of determination, passion and most of all fun! You must have the heart, the mind and in this case, the feet to be able to be successful in the foot modeling industry.

There are some basic routines to have camera ready feet. You must be able to love your feet first before others would want to take a glimpse at them. Loving your feet means taking good care of them by keeping them clean, well groomed and healthy looking. At a minimum, you will be required to have weekly pedicures and make it a point to have a foot scrub and spa every month. An awesome resource I found online is _Treat Your Feet: Exercises To Treat And Prevent Common Foot Ailments_[28]. The book offers Stretching And Strengthening Exercises To Help Relieve Bunions, Hammertoes, Arthritis, Fasciitis, Tendonitis, Tension, In The Feet. Also Aging Feet Exercises To Help Promote Balance And Body Awareness.

You can experiment with all sorts of available services from commercial foot spas which offer foot scrubs with natural concoctions like coffee, salt, and sugar. Some women complain that they have problems with their feet always sweating, even in the winter time. On the website, _CureMySweatyFeet.com_[29] they claim to have a cure for sweaty feet within five days!

Engaging in regular foot massages will also help in the blood circulation which in turn will keep your feet glowing healthy. Remember that your feet bear your weight most of the day, so they need a lot of rest and pampering. Just like a model who needs to feel and look good, ample rest is also needed.

Digital Sex Work:

To be able to have that foot goddess look and feel would mean taking extra measures of vanity for your feet. Some accessories like *toe rings*[30] and stylish footwear go a long way to have that foot goddess appearance. Some *bold nail colors*[31] that exudes a sense of sexiness and desire would surely be a turn on for foot worshipers and a lot of self esteem boosters for foot goddess aspirants.

Developing Your Foot Fetish Theme

Types of Foot Fetishes

There are so many different foot fetish categories for a foot lover to choose from. However, the most successful foot Goddesses I studied, all have a theme or a uniqueness to or about their feet, photos and videos whether it is deliberate or not such as a Latin hotty from Mogi-Guaçu, Sao Paulo, Brazil; Fernanda Amarante. Her foot Goddess brand loves to show off her sexy sandals, bare feet and mesmerizing eyes! Check her out on *Facebook*[32] and her tribute spread on *Sacramentofootfactory's Blog*[33].

If you happen to have long toenails, check out *Cindy Ray's*[34] size 10'S. She is best known as the "ukfootMistress" and the "ArchAngel". Hailing from the Kingston upon Thames, United Kingdom, Cindy Ray is a sophisticated foot Goddess, standing 5' 11". This amazonian foot Goddess says, *"My beautiful stockinged feet, I am truly an Amazon Goddess put on this planet to be worshiped. I love to watch men groveling before me as they humbly worship my beautiful size 8 feet with their high arches, silky-smooth soles and immaculately pedicured and polished natural long, strong toe nails."*

Follow Goddess Cindy Ready:

Instagram[35]

Website 1[36]

Website 2[37]

Clipstore[38]

Email[39]

Digital Sex Work:

Another long toenail internet favorite is international foot Goddesses, *Rainha Grazi*[40] from Florianópolis, Santa Catarina in Brazil. Grazi is a size 10, self proclaimed experienced professional dominatrix, who enjoys a lifestyle of female superiority and supremacy. She says, "*I believe that men have a masculine primitive sexual desire that should be exploited by women. I love having men on my feet. I enjoy using all different kind of sexy sandals, especially sandals that make my feet smell, just to have my slaves sniff and lick my feet and suck my toes. I take very good care of my feet, I always love them to be well pedicured, massaged and worshiped.*"

On her *website*[41], you will find all kinds of fetish content, high-res videos and photos of foot fetish, male humiliation and domination. Goddess Grazi says, "I love men who know how to worship me, spoil me with their money and gifts. I order you to join my website now, I know you will be addicted to me."

Follow Goddess Grazi:

Twitter[42]

Facebook[43]

Youtube[44]

Flickr[45]

Blogspot[46]

Instagram[47]

Another foot fetish theme that remains popular is *toe rings*[48]. Toe rings have been around for years, and have become mainstream for the trend setters and foot lovers. On the sexual side, toe rings are a point of interest for the foot fetish. There is nothing like staring at a well pedicured foot adorned with the perfect toe ring.

What better way to add to the pleasure of a pedicure and foot massage than with foot jewelry of course! Toe rings are usually worn on the second toe, but you may wear them on any or all of your toes; it's a matter of preference. Famous celebrities like Kim Kardashian and *Britney Spears*[49] are famous for putting their best foot forward with their toe ring bling!.

Digital Sex Work:

Toe rings are now gaining new popularity, especially with the younger generation of foot fashionistas. Just like all fashion trends, this is the group that usually dictates what's hot and what's not in the fashion industry. There are a number of shops that sell all kinds of toe rings; the most popular online retailer is *ToeRings.com*[50]. Toe rings could be made of metal, gold and silver and may be worn on any toe as a perfect expression of individuality.

Here are some other popular foot fetish themes: *barefoot sandals*[51], *foot worship*[52], *dirty feet*[53], *soles*[54], *mules*[55], *flip flops*[56], *self toe sucking*[57], *toe licking*[58], *BBW (Big Beautiful Women)*[59], *pantyhose & stocking feet*[60], *celebrity feet*[61], *pedicure feet*[62], *painted toes*[63], *sexy shoes*[64], *toes & soles*[65], and countless others!

Ethnic Foot Fetishes: What Is The Obsession With Asian Feet?

It cannot be denied and hard to ignore; there is indeed a fondness for *Asian women's cute sexy feet*[66]. Call it Asian Fever, Yellow Fever or *Asian Fetish*[67] if you will. Wikipedia defines it as a slang term which usually refers to an interest, strong attraction or preference for people, culture, or things of Asian or origin by those of non-Asian descent.

Some men are very fond of Asian women with their cute sexy build and innocent look. Western men find Asian women alluring and exotic and when it comes to sexual play, Asian women offer a variety of sexual moves that Western men find irresistible.

The desire and fondness for *Asian women's feet*[68] can be attributed to the fact that men get so turned on when they see an Asian woman giggle and moan with pleasure when their feet gets the attention. Asian women's feet also look, feel and taste exotic and sensual because they are smaller in size compared to western women's feet.

Indian Feet & The Beauty of Indian Henna Foot Designs

Temporary tattoos like *Henna*[69] are forms of self expression and design. Henna tattoos also called Mehndi came from the South Asian tradition which uses the henna plant paste. This form of art has been used in various cultures during special occasions like weddings wherein elaborate and intricate designs are being done to the body as a canvass. The feet and hands are the most favorite part, being the ones that are exposed when dressed up. Depending on how complex or simple the designs are, henna tattoos says a lot about the person who wears them.

Internet sources shows a very wide *variety of designs*[70] which are very appealing. With some emphasis on the foot being the body part which can be best showcased. With the advent of these beautiful forms of art, the beautifully tattooed foot is often first to be admired. *Henna foot designs*[71] are exceptionally great because it allows for a limited area of an irregular and live canvas. Depending on the length and color of the foot, plus the shape of the toes, the tattoo artist can "play" the henna designs based on the individuals body or foot structure. What is more appealing are the flowers, animals and shapes that seemed to flow out naturally from the feet, like a continuation of the actual body part. Henna foot designs are most always designs which are nature inspired, or at least most of the time, it goes well with the natural look of the bare legs and feet.

Using a variety of black, brown, red and even orange colors and designs, the tattoo artist blends a henna paste into the skin with utmost care. It's one form of stain that is ideal to have on your skin as a form of self expression. Henna binds with the keratin component of the skin which lasts for weeks, even up to a month and fades gradually as the skin sheds.

If you want more attention to your feet, *henna foot tattoos*[72] can be a cheap, versatile and artistic way to flaunt those peds. Who would not stare or admire the Henna tattoos on someones feet? Our bodies are a special form of canvass, and since the feet have their own identity unique to the owner, they provide a more personalized and challenging venue for art form expression. The future of henna designs is very promising. With more colors and designs available, women of all ethnicities could be wearing one as part of their personalized accessories.

The Many Colors of Ethnic Feet

Ebony Feet[73]

Digital Sex Work:

Italian Feet[74]

Latina Feet[75]

Lebanese Feet[76]

You get to choose which one of these different types of foot fetish ethnicities you want to promote and earn income from. I would suggest starting with a few simple ones and grow your empire over time.

Softcore vs. Hardcore

You can choose to launch a hardcore foot fetish site/blog or a softcore site/blog. I would recommend starting out with softcore because there is less risk than launching a full-fledge, hardcore foot fetish blog/website which will fall under the category of porn!

Remember, once it is out there; you can't necessarily take it back. So, don't consider running for public office, becoming *Miss America*[77] or a CNN News Anchor if you plan to publish hard core, *feet with face*[78] pics and videos.

BTW, you can always make money in the hardcore arena using various affiliate foot fetish sites, products and services. I'll show you how later in the book!

Feet with Face or Just Feet?

Just as you give thought to launching a hardcore or softcore foot fetish empire, you need to also consider your brand and anonymity. If you are going to become a doctor, lawyer or anyone in the public eye that's not in the entertainment business; you may want to consider launching a feet without face website/blog which just shows your feet and legs only and never your face.

However, if you want to play full out and become what's known as a Foot Goddess, then you should look at the benefits of launching a "*feet with face*[79]" foot fetish website/blog. For one, there is a trust value when someone can see your face and know your true identity. But if your feet are so beautiful and your pics and vids are well done, you could easily get away with never showing your face and still earning a living!

Choose Your Online Publishing Platform(s)

One of the questions I always get asked from Foot Fetish Goddesses in embryo is "Do I Need A Traditional Website?"

The quick and decisive answer is, "NO!"

I will qualify that no by introducing you to the most popular website platforms which are free website building tools and platforms such as weebly.com, tumblr.com, wix.com, blogger or even the free version of Wordpress such as the one I use for *Sacramento Foot Fetish Factory*[80]. An example of using Blogger is from *Geisha Kia*[81] or *Tiffany's Tumblr*[82]. I also like this one by *Indian Female Feet*.

You can publish your foot fetish online empire using several online publishing platforms which I highly recommend. However, if this is your first time and you are just starting out, I recommend choosing and mastering just one platform before launching a series of them.

The two most popular publishing platforms is Blogging or a hosted Wordpress website at *Wordpress.org*[83]. An estimated 17% of all the websites in the world run on WordPress or use a customized WordPress framework.

However, the free version of wordpress does not allow you to monetize using affiliate links or shopping cart links on your site and if they find out that you are selling on their free platform, they will shut you down.

The best way to use a free website platform is to use it to promote your free content and point those links to your "money site" or your foot fetish blog/site where you will charge for services or paraphernalia.

Digital Sex Work:

Setting Up Your Wordpress Foot Fetish Blog

STEP ONE (1):

Register the domain name of your foot fetish money site and choose a moderate to low hosting package.

For privacy, I recommend producing a private domain registration. Three of my favorite domain registering and hosting sites are *BlueHost.com*[84], Go Daddy and *HostGator*[85].

STEP TWO (2):

Although, I do not have time to go into how to Install a full Wordpress CMS Platform with a CPanel user interface, I would recommend watching, HostGator's *cpanel overview*[86].

Wordpress Installation

Watch How To Install Wordpress Through Cpanel - *Wordpress Cpanel Install*[87]

Using cPanel with WordPress Website Hosting[88]

How to Set Up a Hosted WordPress Site[89]

Again, later in the book, I'm going to show you how to launch your foot fetish empire without a hosted website or in conjunction with one so there is no excuse for you not to be successful.

The Free Site vs. Fee Site

Foot fetish lovers spend countless hours a day searching for free foot fetish pics and vids. However, many of these surfers are willing to make a purchase if it speaks to their unique kink or foot fetish needs or enhances their personal intimacy in some way. Therefore, you should have a mixture of both free and fee content on your website/blog. So, here's what I suggest...

Digital Sex Work:

Tease With Free To Get Your Fee!

You could produce a free content site/blog or social media space that lures foot fetish prospects to want to buy your personal or custom pics, videos and content.

To cut down on cost and programming, I recommend using free content to promote your foot fetish affiliate products/services also. This offers the foot fetish surfer the best of both worlds. They will become a loyal supporter and follower of your content and trust that you will have complimentary affiliate products/services to peruse at their leisure.

More on this money maker in Chapter 4!

Digital Sex Work:

CHAPTER 2

Best Types of Pics, Vids and Shoes

PICS

There are countless poses, props and positions for you to choose or create; especially if you are modeling new shoes such as flip flops, mules, slides and sandals.

Shoe modeling alone would give you a great reason to buy those new shoes you've been wanting in the store window right?

Kat Kidwell, owner of the Kitty Kat Closett in Pete, Florida offers her unique insight and perspective on the importance of shoes for the foot fetish model in my one-on-one, Q&A:

Q- How do you feel about the moral and ethics of being a foot goddess and having men pay to play with your feet?

A- What's your credit card number……… lol

Q- What are some of the best shoes for women to wear for their foot fetish shoot?

A- HEELS HEELS HEELS!

Q- What are your thoughts about mules, kitten heel thongs or flip flops?

A- Mules are shoes that are more worn for comfort / Kitten heel thongs are worn for sexiness / flip flops worn for running around

Q- What is your favorite shoe to wear?

A- All the above shoes are different many styles, designs, and wear differently. I personally LOVE stilettos... I like them high they make me feel sexy, powerful, and confident.

Q- What is the optimal heel height for a woman choosing shoes for her foot fetish photo and video session?

Digital Sex Work:

A- I personally wear 5-6 inches, but depends how comfortable a women feels in the height.

Q- What are some of the best colors of shoes to wear when taking pics for your foot fetish site?
A- Red/ Hot Pink/ Yellow/ Gold/Black/ Teal/ Orange/ Purple.

Q- When shooting video, which type of shoes make the most provocative sound when walking?
A- When walking, flip flops make the most sound, BUT heels on a hardwood floor sexy!

Q- Why is the sound of soles being slapped by strapless shoes is so erotic?
A- It sounds like skin slapping and reminds you of sex!

Q- Should a foot fetish model match her toenail color to her shoes?
A- NO, if you are wearing a black peep toe heel, red nails give it that sexy pop.

Q- Why do you think men enjoy toe cleavage?
A- Its just like breast cleavage, somewhere to stick something between...LOL

Q- What advice would you give amateur foot models wanting to launch their own foot fetish empire?
A- Do what makes you happy. Be safe, smart, and know men like what they like.

Q- Do you think foot fetishism is a form of sexual expression?
A- I do. I think anything that gives you pleasure is a form of sexual expression.

Q- What is your favorite foot lotion?
A- _Victoria Secret Blush_[90].

Digital Sex Work:

Q- What is the name of your boutique?
A- *Kitty Kat Closet Consignment & Boutique.*

Q- Why did you decide to launch a boutique for BBW's?
A- *I have always felt that society feels like BBW's are unable to be sexy. The clothes that are sold at some of the top retailers are made "grandma" style and the items that are somewhat appealing cost an arm and a leg (and foot, LOL)!*

I have always been asked where do you get this and that from? I shop so much that it is unknown where I was getting things. I normally wear something once and have grown from a one sided closet into a two bedroom dressing room. I got the idea to share my wonderful findings with some of my fellow BBW's.

I have always prided myself on being outside of the box, I believe I am sexy, and confident; even though I am in double digit clothing sizes. I love seeing the look on the ladies faces when they find that one treasure that makes them feel SEXY!

Q- What is your contact info for the readers of this book?
A- *5208 66TH Street North St. Pete, FL 33709*
[Facebook](#)[91], [Pinterest](#)[92], [Twitter](#)[93] : *Kitty Kat Closett*
727-687-6676

Flipinista: A Woman's BFF "Best Flip Flop"

Seriously, ladies, can you ever live without flip-flops? Of course, you cannot! Over the years, these comfortable open-toed rubber flats have become a staple in our getups. They add more character to our maxis, they incorporate style when we're on the beach, and they become are best friends as we traverse unchartered roads when we're out on the holidays.

But here's the thing about flip flops: they can be very boring. Save for a myriad of colors to choose from and straps that are of another shade than the slippers themselves, there's not much done on them—not until Monique Friedman came up with Filipinista.

Digital Sex Work:

Who Is Monique Friedman?

Monique Friedman is an artsy fashionable woman behind the latest fashion trend in the market today: haute couture flip flops. She uses her keen sense of style and great love for flip flops and design to come up with extremely gorgeous pieces you'd surely love to wear all the time. Her flip flops are deeply inspired by many beautiful things and fashion icons such as Valentino, Gucci, Chanel, and Louis Vuitton.

The Many Grand Things about Flipinista

Friedman pours hours and even days crafting the best pair for her clients. In turn, she produces nothing but the best pair of flip flops you can lay your eyes on. Every pair is sourced out from Brazil, the same country where some of the most comfortable and toughest pairs of flip-flops come from. They are made of genuine rubber, so they are definitely flexible and soft on the feet. Further, with proper care, they are going to last for many years.

She also sources out the most classic and pretty pieces of Swarovski crystals, beads, pearls, gems, and other trinkets or charms she patiently sews on the flip flops—yes, these are hand-made stylish, chic slippers, a pure symbol of great love and passion for her art.

To make things even more special, she customizes these slippers according to your own preference. Every pair therefore is a certified standout and 100 percent unique.

Invest in a Good Fashion Statement

Every flip flop is currently sold at around $82 to $92, depending on the style, and boy you've got a lot to pick. You can have the sultry black kitten heel thongs, the beach-y Crystal Heart white flip-flop, the bold and fun sea-inspired pink pair, or the darling Magical Flight. Friedman has also come up with equally charming pairs for the little ladies, such as Hello Kitty.

Flipinista is a hit not only to the women but also the good boys who love to shower their lady loves, from their moms to their spouses, with presents.

Digital Sex Work:

There are thousands of flip-flops out there, but only very few know how to stand out in style. Flipinista combines comfort and fashion and does it so wonderfully you won't be afraid to call it your new best friend.

Check out the latest Flipinista collection at *Friedman's Etsy Shop*[94]. You can also add her in *Pinterest*[95] and *Twitter*[96] so you'll never miss any new design).

So, between shooting pics of your bare feet, soles, painted toenails, and various open toed shoes, you can also pose various foot jewelry such as toe rings, barefoot sandals as mentioned earlier in this book.

Foot Fetish Pics & Vids Examples:

SOLES:
The Soles of Scarlett Maria Ujueta[97]
Vietnam Soles[98]

TOES:
Colorful Toes[99]
Scarlett Maria Ujueta's Colorful Toes[100]

STOCKINGS, PANTYHOSE & SOCKS:
Blue Pantyhose[101]
Great Pantyhose Business Meeting[102]
Fishnets and Pink Polish[103]

MULES, KITTEN HEEL THONGS & FLIP FLOPS:
1 Dollar Thongs To Black Patent Slides[104]
Golden Mules 1[105]
Pedal Pump[106]
Sexy Mules[107]

Digital Sex Work:

Thong sandals flip flop[108]

SELF FOOT WORSHIPING:

HD Feet Heaven[109]

PEDAL PUMPING, CRUSHING & TRAMPLING:

Glasses Crush2[110]

Pedal Pumping[111]

CANDID FEET:

Thong Sandals with Nice Pedi[112]

DIPPING, DANGLING & SHOE PLAY:

Sexy Feet Dangling in White Mules[113]

Flip Flops Dangling[114]

Your Most Controversial or Suggestive Foot Photo Shoot

Considered to be hardcore in the Amateur foot fetish community but, tamer than a full blown foot job is one of the most controversial foot shots or videos you may ever do; the "Creamy Soles" or "Soaked Soles" session. The Creamy Sole shot is a pic or vid of a woman's soles covered or getting covered with semen. Obviously, this would fall into the "hardcore" category but you still have the option of shooting "feet only" and not your face. These types of pic/vids sell for a premium price.

Again, this book is dedicated to the milder, soft core, non-pornographic side of the foot fetish world. You can go as far as you want to. Here are a couple examples of the Creamy Soles shot from *Sacramento Foot Factory*[115].

VIDS

Special Note About Videos:

On all of the Youtube videos recommended in this ebook, the author cannot guarantee that these videos will be available for viewing at time of publication or after as a result of the ever changing policies of youtube — some vids may not be available.

Your First Foot Fetish Video:

Your first video should be an introduction to your feet or foot fetish site/blog. I would then recommend that you plaster that video throughout your social media spaces and make sure you list the URL that points back to your main website/blog to ensure a click through. The goal with an introductory or promotional video is to drive traffic.

Geisha Kia has a great one on her Youtube called "*Meet Kia & Her Feet*[116]." Muscle diva, Latia del Riviero offers a great introduction to her leg and *foot fetish videos*[117], and even has a special gig on Fiverr called, Panthera143 will pics and videos of my feet, and other mild fetishes for $5, only on *fiverr.com*[118].

You Bring me JOI or JOE:

What is it with this you tube sensation that makes it so unbelievably popular? The JOE "Jerk Off Encouragement" or JOI "Jerk Off Instruction" Youtube video sensation in the foot fetish world obviously means giving specific instructions to men on how to cum (or Jerk Off) while staring at the feet of a super hot, foot Goddess, flashing her toes and soles on the screen while verbally arousing the male viewer with words like "*lick my soles, stroke it, suck my toes, cum on my soles.*"

These types of foot fetish videos usually go viral if done well, despite the fact that they go against Youtube's policies. California Feet decided not to give this type of service away for free and charges $14.95 for her 14 minute JOI at *Clips4sale*[119]. Her reason for not posting this type of video on Youtube, she says, "*I refuse to post one on Youtube, as I don't want someone underage to*

Digital Sex Work:

encounter it and that is the reason why I don't talk about my feet in a sexual way on YouTube. I have only made one [Jerk Off Instruction video] which was available on my friends Clips4Sale website and it sold quite a few copies."

Because Youtube frowns upon this type of video, many vids get banned and accounts get closed but, as of the publishing date of this Kindle ebook; with over 400 thousand views, the lovely Anel Orocha100 gives a phenomenal *Sexy Feet JOE*[120].

Producing JOE's or JOI's is soley up to you; pun intended! You can give it away for free on Youtube as a means of driving traffic to your main foot fetish blog site but you must realize that you are not only going against Youtube's policies but allowing underage boys to accidentally discover your video and that could be problematic — legally or morally. Personally, I recommend California Feet's approach; charge a premium for this type of video since you can actually customize it when someone orders it by using their name in the instruction video or just create a generic one that all foot lovers can appreciate.

The Sound of Soles Slapping

As I mentioned in the beginning of this book, one of my true loves is the sound of flip flops or mules slapping the bottom of soft, lickable soles! Every foot lover has their own preference. For me, I love high-heeled or kitten heel thongs and open toed mules. I also like the sound of a woman walking with closed toe mules which causes me to fantasize about the beautiful peds that are hidden from sight.

You could make videos of all the different pairs of shoes you own. There's no limit to the types of photos and/or videos you could shoot.

Pumps are also very sexy as well, especially if there is toe cleavage! If you are going to shoot foot fetish videos, try producing some walking videos and capture the audio sound whereby foot fetish lovers such as myself can hear those heels and soles getting spanked by the bottoms of their open heel shoes. Another term for this type of video is called "Heel Slapping." Below are some examples:

Digital Sex Work:

On Janine Lovesheels' Youtube, she offers *My Day On Mules*[121]. Madiheels' produced "*Walking in High Heel Mules*[122]".

One of my all-time favorite sole slappers is by MrKlepper who uploaded "*Wooden Exercises*[123]". I really like "*Another Sweet Pair of High Heel Mules*[124]" produced by peeptoes1 because its over four minutes long!

Digital Sex Work:

CHAPTER 3

Your At Home Personal Studio

What kind of images should you use — Mobile uploads vs. Studio images?

The power of launching and profiting from your own, personal foot fetish website/blog is that today it is easier than ever to produce a high quality image or video in seconds. You have the power to become the queen of amateur foot fetish.

With your smartphones (or old dumb ones), tablets or digital video cameras, you can launch your very own foot fetish studio. And the fact that it is amateur footage and photos, means you don't have to spend money hiring a production house or photog to do the work. Foot Goddess, California Feet says, "I use a Sony 14 megapixel digital camera and my iPhone 5."

Another resource worth looking into is Iphone Photography Magic - Trick Photography With Your Iphone where you can discover the simple secrets to taking jaw-dropping pictures on your camera phone. I suggest a mixture of both but if you are strapped for cash and time, I would recommend using the mobile phone upload model. It's easy, effective and is the epitome of what an amateur foot fetish site is about.

Not that men don't like highly stylized, posed and professional studio foot fetish images shot by a seasoned photog and model, but there is something that happens in the mind of men when they view an image that looks like it was taken by the girl next door. It seems more personal and intimate which has shown to outsell the professional photo/video sessions by leaps and bounds.

To Light or Not To Light

Depending on your location, you can use daylight and room light to take your foot fetish photos; especially with the technology of a smartphone camera. However, there may be occasions when you want to have better lighting or even lighting. In this case, I would recommend an inexpensive lighting package that you can get on *amazon*[125] for less the a hundred bucks.

Frequency: How Often Should You Produce New Content?

This question is always subjective, however I would recommend at the minimum to produce weekly content if not an upload or two per day.

This will build the anticipatory behavior of your audience/fans and cause them to frequently come back to your site/blog because they expect new content to be there. The reason for setting your timeline and frequency is that eventually your fans will click on one of your affiliate foot fetish links or buy one of your personal digital/physical products.

Most trained foot fetish worshipers are used to daily/weekly content updates. You can try monthly if you have a nice amount of new content that you are uploading but daily updates is highly suggested for those who truly want to live the lifestyle of the rich and famous.

California Feet's California Feet posts her updates using days of the week such as "*Happy Wednesday*[126]".

Digital Sex Work:

CHAPTER 4

Foot Fetish Money Makers

There are several ways for you to make money with your feet.

In many cases, you can launch your own foot fetish empire without ever owning a website/blog or webcam; especially if you use some of the platforms and services featured in this chapter. But first, lets talk about the difference between digital foot fetish products versus physical foot fetish products.

1-PHYSICAL PRODUCTS:

Become open to offering and selling your own foot fetish services, i.e., worn shoes, socks, hosiery!

Yep, there are men and women who would be willing to spend good money on your worn shoes, socks and hosiery and possibly more! For some men, there's nothing like the scent of a woman's worn socks, pantyhose, shoes, etc. As you develop a solid fan base, some of them will want more from you than just some custom pics and/or vids; they want a piece of you! Check out this video from *Isabelle Shy selling her Colin Stuart sandals*[127].

Check out this Flickr Photo Sharing Set of *worn shoes*[128]. On Fetlife, there is an entire group dedicated to selling women's worn shoes called, "Pre Loved" "*Women's Shoes For Sale*[129]". Dixie Perkins out of Kansas City, Missouri launched Goodtimehose on *Facebook*[130] and has not looked back!

It's as simple setting up a free ecommerce system on your site/blog, such as Paypal, 2Checkout.com, Dwolla or Payza.com. If you want to have a sophisticated ecommerce system that includes autoresponders, newsletters and will send "Thank you" messages after each order has been completed, then I recommend setting up a plug-n-play, smart shopping cart system such as *http://www.shockshoppingcart.com*[131] that comes complete with unlimited autoresponders, newsletter templates, and holds up to 10,000 names and email addresses.

Digital Sex Work:

2-DIGITAL PRODUCTS:

Selling your own foot fetish images and videos via email, through your social media network or using platforms such as imgchil or clipstore is a great way to monetize your video and pics efforts such as the *The Foot Geisha*[132], or *Muscle Goddess, Latia Del Riviero*[133]. Hispanic Goddess Camila Mercedes (*Camilafootmode*[134]*l*) is also popular and earning great income.

Another way to earn income for your foot fetish empire is adding the supplementary income garnered from affiliate programs!

3-BECOME AN AFFILIATE OF A FOOT FETISH SITE:

You can do a search on Google, Bing or Yahoo for "foot fetish affiliate programs" and sign up and start immediately selling established foot fetish photos, paraphernalia and more to earn extra income using your site/blog and social media spaces like, Facebook, twitter, etc. You might visit a professional foot fetish site that has an affiliate program, all you have to do is look for a link that usually says, "affiliates" or "webmasters click here".

Why Affiliate Marketing Works

Creating passive income with affiliate marketing can help you reach your financial goals in a very short period of time. The internet has opened up the world to a new kind of advertising that can be very beneficial to all parties involved.

Affiliate marketing is typically based on PPC or PPO. PPC or pay per click means that each time someone visits your site or your blog and they click on an advertisement for a company that you are affiliated with you will collect an agreed upon fee.

PPO pay per order works a bit differently but is usually far more lucrative. The PPO model means that when someone visits your site clicking on the advertisement and following through to the link AND placing the order is when you get paid.

Both cases have their pros and their cons and in either case it is almost like found money because you do nothing more than add a

Digital Sex Work:

link to your site! Affiliate marketing works especially well with niche sites or blogs.

The Necessity of Affiliate Marketing

Thanks to the internet, people are able to find services and goods all around the world. That can be both a positive and a negative!

Many people get frustrated with trying to find simple services in their area because there are too many options. This is where the necessity of affiliate marketing really reveals itself. By both the company and the affiliate offering site visitors an opportunity to explore services and goods that they are interested in (gaged by the content of the site) they are providing a valuable service.

Consumers enjoy being able to visit a familiar site and clicking on goods that are geared toward their interests. For the company the benefit is clear, affiliate marketing drives traffic their way. For the affiliate the benefit is two-fold. They can boost their readership by advertising on their site goods and services that appeal to their audience AND they have the opportunity to make a passive income.

Choosing the Right Company

Half the success in earning a fair passive income from affiliate marketing is knowing what your readership is interested in. There is a good chance that if you have a blog that talks about dogs and you try to sell Zebra herding equipment you are not going to get those clicks.

You have to stay within your readerships interests to be successful.

Here are few of my favorite affiliate foot fetish money making sites:

Feet Jeans[135]

DesignerShoes.com[136]

Feet Factory[137]

I Love Long Toes[138]

LongToes.com[139]

Official Fifty Shades of Grey Sex Toys[140]

Digital Sex Work:

4-SPECIAL REQUEST PICS & VIDS - IN KIND GIFTS & BIG MONEY

Of course you can take tons of photos of your feet and post them to your website for sale, but the real money is in customizing your foot fetish pics and vids by taking on special requests.

Some customers want you to specifically take photos of your feet doing various actions or in specific poses. You determine how far you will go with this since it will be in confidence; especially if it is feet only and your face will not be shown. However, if you are going to take this seriously as a business, you should probably have some legal counsel just to make sure you are not exposed.

Here are a few other ways to specialize your foot fetish content and services:

- Selling special request videos or photos

- Selling foot fetish phone services

- Selling personal request erotic foot fetish stories

- Selling personally worn shoes, socks or stockings

- Create your own Amazon.com Wish List and add the widget or link to your site

5-LAUNCH A CONTINUITY FEET PROGRAM

One of the biggest money-making ventures in the Internet Marketing world is launching membership sites best known as Continuity Programs where visitors become clients by having their credit card debited each month in exchange for specific, exclusive content, services and/or information.

You can also set up an easy subscription-based website, blog or Youtube video by simply producing a subscription e-commerce link using your Paypal dashboard or you can sign up to CC Bill for a more robust subscription-based e-commerce platform. Again, I will highly recommend purchasing a *smart shopping cart*[141] to automate the process whereby you can earn income while you sleep rather than be stuck with the daily details.

Digital Sex Work:

You might find many men/women who will pay you a monthly fee just to talk to you over the phone about their foot fetish needs or send them personal special pics each month exclusively that you could literally take using your phone!

The choice is yours and the options are limitless!

6-FIVERR

Fiverr is the world's largest marketplace for services, starting at $5. Many people didn't know that Fiverr has a naughty side under the categories of "Fun & Bizarre", "Extremely Bizarre" or "Other" where really smart Foot Fetish models offer to paint their toenails any color, send custom photos or videos of their feet, writing your name/company on their feet, wearing any type of shoe you desire and even taking special requests; all for $5!

One of my favorite gigs is having your name, website or company message written on a hot girls feet! Just go to Fiverr.com and type in foot fetish in the search bar and see countless women earning thousands of dollars by selling their feet photos and videos for five dollars a pop!

Here are some of my favorite Fiverr Foot Fetish Gigs:

- *Panthera143 will pics and videos of my feet, and other mild fetishes for $5, only on fiverr.com*[142]

- *Panthera143 will videos of my feet, and other mild related fetishes for $5, only on fiverr.com*[143]

- *Shineykisses will write anything anywhere on my feet for you for $5, only on fiverr.com*[144]

- *Shineykisses will take a video of my feet for $5, only on fiverr.com*[145]

- *Brookevelyn will take pictures of my feet in any way you wish in less than 24 hours for $5, only on fiverr.com*[146]

- *Deadlittlebunny will paint my toes the color of your choice and send you a picture for $5, only on fiverr.com*[147]

Digital Sex Work:

- *Blackbootiegirl will make a 30 second video clip with your name on a sticker and place it between my ebony soles for $5, only on fiverr.com*[148]

- *Bikinigirl will take a picture of my feet with heels or not for $5, only on fiverr.com*[149]

- *Hcpinterns will send you a sexy video tease in black pantyhose nylons for $5, only on fiverr.com*[150]

You can also do a *global search*[151] on Fiverr to get ideas on how foot fetish models are marketing and promoting their Fiverr gigs. Do a Fiverr search result for "foot fetish", "feet" or "shoes".

Its best to have a *Paypal*[152] account or *Dwolla*[153] account setup to have your funds deposited. If you don't have a Paypal, they will send you a check or make other arrangements for you to receive your funds. Fiverr takes $1 from every transaction so you actually earn $4 per gig order. The beauty is you can have several gigs. Some women are earning thousands of dollars a day on Fiverr; you could be one of them!

ACTION STEPS:

Go to *http://www.fiverr.com*[154] and click on the tab, "Start Selling" or "join".

Use a personal email address, username and password and do not connect it or signup using Facebook.

7-AMAZON.COM WISHLIST

One of the smartest ways to make money from your foot fans is setting up an Amazon.con Wish list which costs you nothing but could give you everything!

A wish-list is a simply a list of items sold on Amazon that you choose and desire for someone to gift to you. This used to be exclusive to wedding planners but smart foot fetish marketers are getting hip to how many fans all over the world who have Amazon.com accounts are more than willing to purchase and gift

Digital Sex Work:

you almost anything you desire, as long as it exists in the Amazon.com store.

Additionally, you must create a public wish list and use the URL in your browser as your wish list address. Once you set up your Amazon Wish-list, copy and paste the URL into your website or blog, announce it on your social media channels and watch the gifts start pouring in.

You should have a large variety to things on your wish-list that range in inexpensive to over the top expensive. But make sure it something you actually want and desire.

To give you an idea of how easy it is to earn in-kind gifts, you can check out Patricia Pine's *Amazon.com Wish-list*[155] as an example.

8-CLIPSTORES

According to Suncoast Productions (Owners of Clips4Sale.com), their website is an International Multi-Media online entertainment business which allows producers and sellers to offer clips for sale, images for sale, and videos for sale. The site is dedicated to servicing the adult community with the highest quality products and vendors. It uses 128bit SSL encryption for maximum security. Your information is never sold, shared, or rented. Aside from being a great alternative to high priced rentals, our site provides an excellent marketplace for producers to sell their work.

With the advent of digital videography, and so many people armed with cameras of high enough quality to shoot great videos, we loved the idea of making the media available, at a low price, while providing the producers and sellers the ability to open a studio and be paid a commission for each clip sold. Currently you'll find a large selection of high resolution media on our site, more of which is being added daily.

A Marketplace for Producers

Whether you are a producer or a seller, you can open a studio account, and securely host your media to a broad range of audience. Approved producers and sellers can upload their media to the website or a foot fetish affiliate, and this media can be downloaded

Digital Sex Work:

by other users. Each time media is downloaded, the producer earns revenue as stated in their agreement. When producers have earned at least $100 they can request an ACH payment, wire transfer, or check payment.

True Royalty Payouts

If you are a creator or seller of video media, most services limit your ability to resell your media with their so called "royalty-free" media incentives - but not at our site. Please refer to our Content Providers Agreement and Image Usage Agreement for full details.

Click on "*store info*[156]" to open your own digital download store.

One of my favorite international foot Goddesses from Guayaquil, Ecuador is *Camila Mercedes De Bellucc*[157]*i* who has an awesome catalog of clips on *Clips4sale*[158]. On her intro page she says, *"I'm a Ecuadorian amateur foot model and my photos and videos are taken with sensuality to the right measure. So, If you were looking for beautiful and sexy foot fetish photos and videos, with focus on rich content and image quality, you have come to the right place. Come on inside and take a look at my stunning art."* Camila does not speak English, but her beautiful peds will speak to you regardless! Check out her social spaces at Facebook under "*Camilafootmodel*[159]" and *Twitter*[160].

9-IMGCHILI

With *imgChil*[161]*i* you can earn money sharing your images! imgChili lets you earn cash by sharing images with your family and friends: every time a visitor views one of your images, you are automatically credited with a variable amount of money

While ImgChili is free to use, you can earn up to $3.00/1000 views. Check out their *FAQ*[162] or view a *demo*[163].

If you have an old Flickr account and want to monetize it, just use ImgChili to convert your photos and upload the new thumbnails to your Flickr and remove the freebies!

Digital Sex Work:

You can upload a group of five or more images at a time to ImgChili and it will convert the photo collection to thumbnail html. You can then take that html and paste it into your website.

When a foot fetish clicks on the thumbnail to see the larger picture, they will first be redirected to a live cam site. On that page, there will be a link on the upper left hand corner of the page to click on larger image they were looking for.

When your thumbnail image is clicked on however, you get paid by imgChili via Paypal or Payza. Here is an example *link*[164].

WARNING: imgchili shows graphic webcams in order to monetize their click-through conversion.

10-EBAY

That's right, you can sell your special foot fetish services, pics and paraphernalia on Ebay because they have a special "*Adult Only*[165]" login with a plethora of categories.

Whether it's worn shoes or special request videos and photos; Ebay is yet another resource for you to be able to make money with your feet without owning a website.

According to *HiddenAuctions.com*[166], Ebay does not openly promote their adult section and keeps it hidden from sensitive eyes. However over 73 million people buy and sell adult content on Ebay. If you go to Ebays categories and type in "Everything Else" you will literally find tons of adult and fetish content for sale.

You could easily set up a store and sell your foot fetish paraphernalia such as worn shoes, socks, pantyhose, custom photos, videos, etc.

11-NITEFLIRT

If you have the gift of gab, and love to talk on the phone, you may use your foot fetish powers to seduce men and women by launching your own *Niteflirt*[167] hotline!

Yep, you can Answer the phone, send mails, photos, stories and get paid for the services you provide. Charge the rate that makes sense

Digital Sex Work:

for you. Niteflirt allows you to set your hours to take calls when you want, as often as you want, from anywhere you can answer a phone with the comfort of knowing your personal information is never revealed.

What's also cool about Niteflirt is you can receive a free web site address and toll free 800 number with your own personal extension! You can use their mail service to send personalized marketing email offers, foot fetish, photos, stories to new and existing customers. Best of all, you can add your call button to other web pages and link directly to your listing on NiteFlirt.

Here is an example of Cayenne Soles who has set up her own *Niteflirt business*[168].

12-FOOT FETISH PARTY MODEL

All around the globe at this very second while you are reading this book, there is a foot fetish party happening somewhere in the world!

A foot fetish party is usually done where a group of models with beautiful feet entertain paid guests of the party to worship their feet. Most foot fetish parties is feet only and no sex of any kind; make sure you clarify this with the host of the party if you are looking to be hired for one of these events.

Craig's List and BackPage are the best online classified ads to find such Sex Work.

Here are a few ads I found as examples of what a burgeoning, amateur Foot Goddess can expect:

EXAMPLE 1:

Trick or Treat... Got Smelly Feet? Foot Fetish Modeling (Up to $200 Per 90 Minutes) - 40

CAREFULLY READ THIS ENTIRE AD AND PROVIDE ALL INFORMATION ASKED OR YOU WILL BE DISCONSIDERED

Fetish photographer welcomes females, 18+, with attractive feet and toes for foot fetish still picture and video segment modeling. Plus size, BBW, SSBBW, Black & Latina ladies extremely welcomed!!!

Digital Sex Work:

These cash paid modeling assignments focus on two very specific areas: 1) feet, face & body posing, & 2) foot domination modeling (trampling, standing, stomping & jumping atop another person, martial arts kicking, etc). You will be required for BOTH types of modeling, therefore an open mind and aggressive attitude is a MUST!!!

These projects contain NO nudity and DO NOT require any sexual content WHATSOEVER. Two paid levels are available... one for remaining anonymous, while the other would require face & body recognition (conspicuous).

For additional info, kindly respond to this BackPage ad & be sure to include the following stat info: Your first name (or stage name), age, height, weight, shoe size & width, nationality and location.

BackPage also allows for one small pic to be sent. Please include EITHER a full body shot OR a close-up two feet together shot (as seen in one of the pics to the right).

BackPage's automatic email answer system will immediately send out my more detailed info to you. Please check your spam/junk folders if necessary, as this more detailed info response will have embedded pictures and a link for video clip previews, which can sometimes be filtered and placed in these folders.

Thank you.

• Location: Atlanta, Model Your Feet For $$$

EXAMPLE 2:

Foot fetish models needed! ! ! {NO NUDITY} (Nashville)

Looking for ATTRACTIVE women with nice feet to participate in foot fetish activity. Must be at least 18, all ages and shoe sizes accepted. No nudity required. We can discuss comfort level with various foot fetish themes. If interested please send picture of yourself and contact info. This could potentially be an easy way to supplement your income with a few extra bucks per week with multiple sessions at $100/hr; $50 per 30min. You must be ATTRACTIVE if you're not this ad isn't for you. If you're attractive your sweaty smelly feet are delightfully delicious & desirable. If you're unattractive your sweaty smelly feet are repugnantly revolting & repulsive. YES, there is a double standard. MILF & young girls & all shoes sizes welcome as long as you're ATTRACTIVE! ! ! You don't have to be a super model but at least a 7 on a scale of 1 -10 unanimously by universal standard

EXAMPLE 3:

ElegantBareFeet Foot Fetish Party - Friday, November, 15 2013

Have you ever experience a foot party before? if not.. Then, This is the chance to meet beautiful girls with gorgeous feet. Only in Los Angeles will be hosting a foot party with a few girls ready to have their feet worship by real foot men just like you.

I have attached still images of the ladies that will be attending this event.

For info or details just email. RSVP by going to the site Elegantbarefeet.com

> Tony.
>
> I was so curious about the concept of foot parties that I actually contact Tony Moreno of *ElegantBareFeet.com*[169] conducted a Q&A with him for a better understanding of what a foot model can expect at a Foot Party.
>
> RedPedSole:
>
> When did you start, elegantbarefeet.com?

Tony Moreno:

I started Elegantbarefeet on October 28, 2011, a few days away from Halloween. But, To make the party exciting I had a Halloween theme to it. I went wild having those few sexy ladies that were there with their sexy outfits. Only a hand full of people showed up, But that was expected on that night. That is one special event I will never forget.

Digital Sex Work:

RedPedSole:
What can foot fetish lovers find on the site?

Tony Moreno:
This site caters to foot men who love female feet. Attending to any of our events can have a real experience with any of our females with pretty feet.

RedPedSole:
What is a foot party and foot fun?

Tony Moreno:
A foot party is actually a social gathering for foot fetish people who want to talk about their foot fetish experience and also meet gorgeous females who love to have their feet pampered by foot men.

RedPedSole:
How do you advertise your foot parties?

Tony Moreno:
Any social media where the foot community hang around.

RedPedSole:
How much can an amateur foot model make at a foot party event?

Tony Moreno:
This foot party is like a strip club. Because beauty and a great personality can make them get that cash. But I do not ask all the models how much they make in one night. Although there was this girl who told me that she made around $400.

RedPedSole:
You have a clipstore account; what can we expect to see on there?

Digital Sex Work:

Tony Moreno:

I do have a Clip Store. and what you expect to see is a variety of foot fetish clips.: Foot Worship, POV and foot humiliation.

RedPedSole:

How much do models make from appearing on these videos?

Tony Moreno:

It all depends how good they are in front of the camera. I get girls from newbies to pros and everyone has their talent, From $50 - $300 depending on their skill on camera.

RedPedSole:

Do you do hardcore foot porn or just softcore feet?

Tony Moreno:

For now I only have softcore feet clips. Everything in this clip store is clean and has no nudity or any sexual intercourse. Very soon i will be adding some nude models on my clip store. But I am also interested in doing foot porn in the near future.

RedPedSole:

Is there sex involved at a foot party?

Tony Moreno:

No SEX is allowed at my party.. That is my #1 policy for everyone who step foot at my events. I have to maintain it clean, legal and most of all safe for everyone specially the girls.

RedPedSole:

When did you develop your foot fetish?

Tony Moreno:

I became aware of my foot fetish when I was 4 yrs old! Of course, It wasn't a sexual thing but I just had this weird attraction for feet. Until I hit puberty this foot fetish showed me a whole different feeling... A good feeling!

Digital Sex Work:

RedPedSole:
Why type of feet do you like in particular?

Tony Moreno:
Well, if you referring to the part of the foot I like then I would say the wrinkled soles. That would be my biggest weakness! A sexy young girl with a really light tone skin color that has big feet included with meaty wrinkled soles.

RedPedSole:
Is foot parties and having foot fun a form of prostitution?

Tony Moreno:
As long there is no sexual activity like, intercourse, footjobs, or touching their private parts with their feet. I want this to be legal and legit as possible.

RedPedSole:
Do you have to have a special permit to host a foot party?

Tony Moreno:
No I don't. I think this is why it's called a foot party and I believe that if I would have a permit I would have my own location and be open on regular business hours. Kind of like a strip club. But I sure would love to have something like that. In the near future; an official venue for foot men to go to.

RedPedSole:
Do the models have to be a certain age to participate?

Tony Moreno:
All the models have to be 18 yrs and older. This applies to foot parties and video shoots.

RedPedSole:
How long does a foot party last?

Digital Sex Work:

Tony Moreno:

I always try to make it 5 hours of fun. It starts from 8pm to 12 midnight. There are times people stay till 1am but after that, everyone needs to go home . hehe!

RedPedSole:

What about anonymity? I'm sure some guest would want to keep their identity confidential; are taking photos allowed?

Tony Moreno:

I consider this a private foot party only on special invitation for foot men and women. So everyone who has this fetish can attend. I do take pictures but only to the models. Respecting everyone's privacy is one of my rules.

RedPedSole:

Do you have security at foot party events?

Tony Moreno:

I have a few of my staff that are always on patrol. But so far I haven't had any problems.

RedPedSole:

How many foot models participate at these events and how many men?

Tony Moreno:

Like any other event, the numbers are not always accurate. The most I have got in one night was like 50 people in total and the least was around 10 people. My parties are small so my average number of girls would be around 20. If I get more girls showing up, Good! But there are times when that average number of girls drop. I always get my ups and downs.

RedPedSole:

So, does a guy pay over and above the cover charge to rub/massage a woman's feet?

Digital Sex Work:

Tony Moreno:

Yes, The cover charge to get in is $40 flat. I think i can't get any lower than that. What i am providing with that price is, Sexy young girls who are open-minded about any foot fetish (Foot Worship,Trampling, Foot Smelling, Tickling) , private session booths, Food and non-alcohol drinks, BYOB is allowed.

RedPedSole:

What about cleanliness, how do women keep their feet clean when so many men are licking on them?

Tony Moreno:

I do provide some witch hazels and napkins to disinfect after a good session with a model.

RedPedSole:

Do you have foot parties in different parts of the country and world?

Tony Moreno:

I have always been thinking about doing foot parties somewhere in Texas, Oregon or San Diego. last year I went to Mexico and had that idea in doing a foot party over there. There is a lot of people with foot fetishes around the world.

RedPedSole:

Why do you think foot fetish is becoming so popular?

Tony Moreno:

There are tons of foot fetish websites on the internet. Besides, foot fetish has been mention on the media, TV Shows, Movies, Music even on sports. Today it's easy to talk about foot fetish. 15 yrs ago it wasn't that easy. It used to be one of the weirdest taboo and you could be ridiculed if you exposed your foot fetish to everyone.

Digital Sex Work:

RedPedSole:
Do you think it is the best way to have safe sex?

Tony Moreno:
I think it would be safe sex for the person who has the foot fetish. Most foot men won't even bother having intercourse sex with a lady if her feet is the only sexual contact they prefer. I remember I was that type of guy before.

RedPedSole:
What are your thoughts on women launching their own foot fetish site?

Tony Moreno:
I think there is a small percentage of females that are running their own site, I think they are the ones that are making that fat money. Most of them are selling videos, socks, shoes they even doing private sessions. Some women don't know the power they have just by using their feet. They can make men beg down on their knees and also make that dollar with them.

RedPedSole:
What advice would you give a newbie foot model wanting to launch their own site and begin in the business?

Tony Moreno:
Any girl can be a foot model if you have what guys really like; attractive, beautiful feet and that charming personality. All I know is that this is not for all females out there. I have seen girls who tried to come up but never did. I don't know if it's their feet or their appearance but something was wrong. But if something like this happens to any newbie trying to make it on her own, just get back up and find another way to make foot men drool.

Digital Sex Work:

13-WORK WITH FOOT FETISH PHOTOGRAPHERS

An awesome way to make money as an Amateur Foot Fetish Model is hiring your feet to make money with photographers who are willing to pay you or your feet for your time!

This is an ad I saw on Craig's List:

Looking For FEMALE Models for Foot Fetish Shooting.

No Need Experience.

Included Foot Worship, a Guy Will Kiss and Lick ur Feet On Camera.

Please Add a Pic Of Full Body.

$100 Per Hour With Show Face In Camera.

$50 Per Hour Without Showing Face In Camera.

Must Be 18 And Older.

14-MAILING LIST, AUTORESPONDER AND ECOURSE

Everyone uses email and one of the most important aspects of building your foot fetish empire is learning the process of list building. List building and having a newsletter or communicating with your foot fans with updates, specials and services will guarantee money in your bank account if done correctly and consistently.

Email marketing still remains one of the best methods to generate leads and, later on, customers. According to an Experian study, you get more than 40% return for every dollar you spend on e-mail promotions.

To make sure you succeed, here are steps and tips to remember:

1. Use a reliable e-mail building tool. There are a lot of programs out there that can help you with building an e-mail list, but only a handful of them will be worth your while. Make sure that you get to know the features and find one that is scalable—that is, it grows as your leads also increase.

Digital Sex Work:

2. Make use of an autoresponder. You only have a few-second window before your leads start thinking that newsletter is bogus. That's why it's imperative that you have an autoresponder. You need to have an autoresponder which will reply back automatically to a new subscriber with a personal "thank you" email when they optin to your mailing list. After that the thank you email is sent, you can load and set the autoresponder to send out automated updates to your list without having to physically push the button or sit in front of your computer. That is why it is called an autoresponder; it responds automatically to those on your list.

So far, *Aweber*[170] is one of the most trusted programs out there, but there are a few strong competitors. It's best you compare their features and benefits to find one that suits your needs.

Even if mailing list programs have gone cheap for the past few years, they still cost you something. If you fail to choose the right one, you're just wasting your hard-earned money, which could have been used for other business-related expenses.

Fortunately, you have options like *YourMailingListProvide*[171]*r* that lets you test the system first before you eventually choose your plan. The free trial entitles you up to 25 entries in the mailing list. It is consumable at any time. Once all of them have been consumed, you will be prompted to choose any of the affordable packages offered by the company.

It's also easy and fast to sign up. You just need to input your e-mail address and the access code, which is represented by a series of numbers you see on the screen. This is needed to prevent any automated signups. You also need to agree with the terms and conditions and the Anti-spam Policy. Take note that the United States has a law against spamming.

YourMailingListProvider doesn't bombard you with plenty of choices to speed up the selection process. Currently there are three: free, Pro, and Pro Plus.

The free option means that you don't have to pay for anything at all, but you're still entitled to a lot of features such as e-mail newsletter builder, template gallery, social media integration, and Google

Digital Sex Work:

Analytics integration. You can also create both public and newsletter archives, bounceback reports, and API automation. Nevertheless, there are limitations. For example, your total number of signups can only be up to a thousand.

For a more scalable approach, choose either Pro or Pro Plus. Both allow you to add unlimited leads into the mailing list. Pro costs only $3.75 per month and lets you import contacts from address books easily. You can also generate a report of the click-through and open rates. Pro Plus, meanwhile, is $5 per month, with advanced reporting on activities per contact.

3. Create a strong headline. More than 30 percent of recipients open their mails based on the headline or subject. After all, it's the first thing they see when they check their inbox. Drafting the best subject can be tricky as you don''t want to be too vague they don't really get what the mail is about or too specific it removes the fun of opening it. It's advisable therefore to create at least 3 to 5 subjects first and choose the best.

4. Give more value to your e-mails. One of the reasons why they're subscribed to you is because they're expecting value. You thus have to give it to them. Provide them fresh new information about the subject, share success stories, and, most of all, use the chance to promote your products and services by perhaps giving away coupons, discounts, and other offers exclusive to e-mail subscribers. According to Blue Kangaroo Study, around 70 percent had utilized a coupon they got from an e-mail.

5. Let them share content. By including social media buttons or URL's in your e-mail, you are actually increasing your click-through rate to as high as 158 percent.

6. Lead them to the other parts of the sales funnel. Don't hard sell, but also don't let go of the opportunity to get them to buy something or move on to the other sections of what you have for sale and to offer. Use your mailing list to entice foot fetish fans to sign up for more offers, try out samples, or even shop during sales.

Digital Sex Work:

7. Keep it brief but concise. Readers don't have the time to read lengthy landing pages and e-mails. Go straight to the point, but make sure you cover all the bases.

How to Produce an E-course:

An e-course is one of the information products that can help increase your income to a thousandfold. But more than anything else, it allows you to impart learning to others and make an impact into their lives by the information you share.

But how do you make one? Here are some of the essential steps:

1. Know your subject. Just like when you are in college, your e-course should be subject-centric, and it helps if it is as specific as possible. For example, if your topic is about blogging, perhaps the e-course will be about how to blog and earn money out of it. Although you can already write an e-course in almost any subject since you have access to a wide variety of materials today, it is still ideal if you write something that you know by heart. This lets you share information not found in any other e-course. You can also have a better idea of the direction of your e-course when you have an authority over your subject.

2. Determine if it is for free or not. An e-course can be given away for free, as a way of saying thank you to your subscribers as well as to add value to your main offer. It can also be your bread and butter. Nevertheless, it is essential to know what it really is to you as it informs you of the length. A free e-course is normally good for a couple of days or at most a week. A regularly paid e-course can last for several weeks or months.

3. Create the outline. The outline basically tells you the subjects that will be tackled in every release. Some writers prefer to write everything first and then divide the entire course into small parts. Regardless, by having an outline, you will have a clearer idea on what kinds of data to look for, how to present such information, and how to enhance the flow of the learning process.

4. Identify your channels. How are you going to distribute the e-course? Often, e-learners subscribe to the course through their e-mail. This means the materials are sent into their inbox. There are

also others who set up a dedicated website. Those who have paid for the course can log in and download the materials from there. You can also diversify your e-course to include podcasts and videos, among others.

5. Make the e-courses more dynamic. We all want variety once in a while, especially when we are trying to learn something. It will greatly help your students if you can make the subject matter more dynamic or interactive. Schedule tele-seminars or webinars, let them take quizzes or submit assignments, or encourage the creation of a community where they can share learning.

6. Be open for feedback. You want your e-course to be helpful, useful, and appreciated. To know if you achieve your goal, allow your e-learners to send you feedback. You can also send a survey or questionnaire once in a while.

15-EBANNED

WARNING: This Site Contains Material For Mature Adults Only!

Ebanned.net[172] is touted as the only Premier Adult Trading Community and Auction Site in the world! They allow you to bid or buy XXX movies, used panties, amateur photos, pic collections and more! Established in November 2000, Ebanned offers a lot more flexibility than Ebay because it is a bidding platform exclusively for the fetish, kink community. You could literally have thousands of people bidding to buy your using stockings, shoes, socks, foot pics, videos and more. Imagine the possibilities!

16-BECOME A FOOTDOM

Becoming a Foot Dominatrix can be extremely profitable and rewarding. Would you believe that there are men across the globe; some who are very rich that would fly in to your city just to suck, lick and worship your feet?

There are some men who are die hard foot slaves and love to be humiliated and dominated by their personal footdom, telling them, making them, forcing them to suck and lick your feet. You must develop the personality and language that will turn these type of men on but the financial reward outbids the necessary learning curve.

WARNING: Be careful when you launch this part of your foot fetish business as there are quite a few idiots out there. The experts say you should have a male escort to accompany you while engaging in this type of foot fetish business. You should thoroughly screen the foot fan before meeting anyone.

17-WEBCAM WORK

Using your laptop or desktop webcam or even the webcam on your tablet, you could launch a roaring foot fetish business simply by charging for 5, 10, 15 or 20 minute foot fetish sessions! California Feet charges around $50 per session but you get to set your own price!

This is becoming one of the most popular ways of appeasing the foot fetish fan because it is as close to a live session as you get without physical contact. It also breaks down the barrier of geography and distance. You can or your foot fan can be anywhere in the world and you can serve up a good digital dose of toes, soles and more for your client. There are many webcam services you can use but most foot goddesses charge up front using paypal and use skype to deliver their digital foot connection.

WARNING: When conducting webcam foot fetish session; be discreet about what you have in the background of your camera so that there is nothing unique that will identify where you live or would be easily recognizable in public. Also, don't give out personal information such as your address, cell #, etc.

Once you have implemented one or all of the aforementioned foot fetish money makers, it is then time to start implementing a social media campaign to properly promote your burgeoning foot fetish empire. But first, read Amateur Foot Fetish Goddess, Patricia Pine's Q&A to gain more ideas and insight on how to become your own foot fetish mogul!

Digital Sex Work:

18-ADULTWORK.COM REVIEW

AdultWork.com – Your Source for Adult Service Providers, Erotic Content and Live Cams

The idea behind *AdultWork.com*[173] is simple: it's a place where those who offer adult content and those who subscribe to it can gather. At this point, the site can be called a community just because of a shared interest. Although the overall theme of the site may not be looked kindly upon, it does cater to a certain need.

A lot of people make use of AdultWork.com for a number of reasons. Some use it as a source of income. Others use it to fulfill a certain need. Whichever type of user you are, you will find a lot of services that answer your needs at AdultWork.com.

All this said, what can AdultWork do for its users?

For adult content providers

It is an anonymous platform for providing adult-related services. On their homepage, AdultWork.com states that it "is committed to providing a safe and anonymous environment where individuals can distribute and market their own products, services and content." A lot of people value anonymity in these days of digital exposure, especially those who choose this way of earning money. It's understandable why they would want to hide their true identity and AdultWork.com provides just that.

It allows users to build an adult-themed store. You can sell adult-related products on AdultWork. It is not solely restricted to those who want to offer services, but those who want to sell products for clients and for users of the site as well. Some examples of adult-themed products that can be seen on the site are dildos, cigarettes and fetish items.

It has a large amount of traffic. AdultWork receives its fair share of visitors who are looking for different things. There's a high chance to book a client if your services fit with certain needs. For example, if others who provide the same services as you are booked, there's a huge chance that your services will be acquired instead.

Digital Sex Work:

It offers several categories for sharing content. Whatever kind of content users want to consume – photos or videos – and even talking through the phone or chat are all available. In case you want to do business in something adult-related, know that you have lots of options at AdultWork. If you're not too comfortable with posting sexy pictures, you can opt to have a chat either through the phone or chat with a client instead.

Above all things, you get paid for whatever services you provide through the site.

For adult content consumers

It allows users to anonymously fulfill a need. Whether you're the curious type or are looking for company, AdultWork provides you with an anonymous and safe platform where you can make this possible. The site does not require you to use your real name or address. Rather, you're free to make an account that is solely specific for accessing AdultWork.

It allows users to choose from a wide variety of providers. There are lots of users who offer services on AdultWork and you can choose which ones suits your best by taking a good look at their profile. It's important that you do this so you don't get scammed.

It allows you to consume various kinds of content. Whether you choose to view pictures or watch videos, AdultWork offers you a variety of content to choose from. Whatever form of content you prefer, there's a platform on AdultWork that offers what you need. Be it just talking on the phone or chatting, there are providers on AdultWork for you.

AdultWork caters both to those who seek and create adult-related content. Not just that, users – both creators and searchers – are not required to reveal their identity which gives each one total anonymity.

CHAPTER 5

Promoting Your Foot Fetish Empire

How To Create A Social Surge:

I have discovered there are four social signals that are best to use to promote your foot fetish site; Facebook, Youtube, Twitter and Pinterest.

However, there are several other communities that you need to join and become active in if you are going to truly saturate the foot fetish ethers. For example, if you decided to use Youtube as one of your main social platforms, I suggest that you create a weekly series of short YT videos (2-5 minutes) and use Twitter, Facebook and/or Pinterest to promote the YT link. This keeps your content fresh and keeps return worshipers coming back while attracting and creating many new ones.

But for now, let me teach you how to…

Find, Create and Build Your Foot Fetish Community

FETLIFE

One of my favorite foot fetish communities is *Fetlife.com*[174]. Here you can create a profile, upload photos and videos, interact with other like minded foot fetish's and drive traffic back to your website and social media signals.

Fetlife allows you to upload video, photos and links back to your foot fetish money site as well as write erotic stories and have them posted throughout the Fetlife community. The smart thing to do is put all of the links in your profile from your other foot fetish sites. Everything should be interconnected so that your potential foot fan becomes lost in your foot fetish empire and becomes a lifelong fan and funder!

Another smart use of Fetlife is to looking into their advertising system which is similar to Facebook. Just visit *Fetlife Ads*[175] and

Digital Sex Work:

read the benefits of advertising your foot fetish sites and watch the profits start coming in.

BTW, you can type in RedPedSole and see my profile on Fetlife and become a foot friend in kink!

WARNING - Fetlife.com is a full on kink site and there is nothing holding anyone back. You will see a lot more than just feet so be cool!

FACEBOOK: (PERSONAL ACCOUNT)

On Facebook, Patricia Pine who was featured in the Q&A interview at the beginning of the book and who's photos are shown throughout this ebook, has another account exclusively for her foot fetish fans called, *Patrica Pine*[176].

I would recommend setting up another account with perhaps your stage name and a different email address and phone number if you can. This only applies if you are making the effort to keep your personal life separate from your business life; otherwise, why bother?

FACEBOOK: (PAGES)

You can also launch as many Facebook Pages as you like and update regularly to promote new content you have uploaded to your foot fetish money site. Although, 90% of people once they click your LIKE button on FB never return, foot fetish lovers are different and will return if you are posting on a regular basis and posting hot foot fetish images.

Here are a few of my personal Facebook Favorites:

The Sole Lounge[177]

Red Ped Sole[178]

We Love Womens Feet[179]

My Feet Fetish[180]

Feet Lovers Tunisia[181]

Digital Sex Work:

I Love Feet Nails[182]

Natasha Lov Feett[183]

Lynn Jones[184]

Foot Fetish Videos[185]

Cayenne Soles[186]

Natasha Lov Feet[187]

Feet Licking[188]

Hot Facebook Tips:

- 80 characters or less gets the highest click through

- Post less frequently such as once or twice a day.

- Photos, video gets better CTR than links.

- Use full links verses short links.

- The best time to post on Facebook is 10am EST to 4pm EST or 7am PST to 1pm PST

- Thursday and Friday gets the best engagement rate; about 18% higher

- Post manually on Facebook verses using automated services such as hootsuite or marketmesuite

- Create a post on FB; shorten the link and post it on twitter. This will gently direct people to your fan page without asking them to do so.

Always leave your Facebook Page or Blog URL (http:// included) in the front of any post or status update you participate in.

FACEBOOK: (GROUPS)

As an alternative to a page, you can also launch your own Facebook Group and control who gets access. In the foot fetish community, Facebook Groups are extremely popular! They are also good for selling physical products such as worn shoes, socks, pantyhose, etc.

Digital Sex Work:

If you are just using Facebook to join groups to promote your foot fetish site then as always, introduce yourself to the new community but don't spam them with your photos and links until you have at least said hello.

Leave a message, acknowledge that you are new to the community and begin a sincere dialog with the folk there. This will go a long way in terms of building up your social foot fetish community.

FEETWIN

Feetwin.com[189] is a Foot Fetish Social Network and one of my Fetlife friends, "*ToeBunny*[190]" hipped me to this community and I *joined immediately*[191] and highly recommend it for those serious about penetrating the foot fetish community.

A great benefit to joining the Feetwin community is they have a *blogging platform*[192] which could work wonders for back links and driving traffic back to your paid sites. You can also upload tons of photos, videos, engage in their forum and even connect your websites "rss feed" and more!

TUMBLR

Tumblr.com[193] is another great social platform to share and promote your free photos/videos to promote and direct potential fans to your paid foot fetish site.

Check out this great "*How To*[194]" video explaining how to set up a Tumblr account.

Tumblr Example:

I am a 25 year old girl called *Tiffan*[195]*y* living and working somewhere in the south of Europe ;) Absolutely in love with feet and knowing there are many out there like me I have decided to share my fetish with you. I love nice high heels/boots and surprising my bf with foot jobs. He loves smelling my feet either after a long day at the office in my stockings or just barefoot in boots. His tongue tickles my toes every time he decides to kiss and lick them. Hope you all enjoy my blog and there is lots to come! xxx

Digital Sex Work:

YAHOO GROUPS

Similar to Facebook Groups, the rules are the same. Find out what the rules are before you begin posting. Then use some of your free images/videos to promote your foot fetish money site.

CRAIGSLIST

Craigslist is an awesome way to get men and women to tune into your feet by posting ads in the personals to direct foot fetish lovers to your web page, blog, video, etc.

Here is an ad example I have shared with many up and coming foot fetish goddesses to successfully promote their blog:

[AD EXAMPLE]:

Subject Line:

Looking for men who will adore my beautiful feet

Body Text:

Hi,

I'm launching my very own foot fetish site and would like to invite you to review my feet for free before the site turns into a paid site.

All you have to do is adore my beautiful feet and leave a positive review.

Can you do that? You may get an extra treat if you are obedient!

TWITTER

When sending out tweets about your feets; (LOL) be sure to use these powerful Hashtags to ensure your tweets go viral.

What are Hashtags?

Hashtags[196]

According to *Wikipedia*[197], A hashtag is a word or a phrase prefixed with the symbol #. It is a form of metadata tag. Short messages on micro blogging and social networking services such as Twitter, Tout, identi.ca, Tumblr, Instagram, Flickr, Google+ or Facebook

Digital Sex Work:

may be tagged by putting "#" before important words, as in: #FF which stands for "Follow Friday."

Hashtags provide a means of grouping such messages, since one can search for the hashtag and get the set of messages that contain it.

You can use as many hashtags as you want so long as they fit within the twitter format of 140 characters or less. Hashtags also work with Instagram to help foot fetish followers easily search and group their favorite content.

Here is a list of the best foot fetish hashtags to use with your status updates.

#feet, #foot , #toes , #feetstagram , #instafeet , #footlove , #feetlove , #feetdream , #toebabe , #footfetish, #cutefeet , #cutetoes , #sexyfeet , #sexytoes, #perfectfeet , #pedi, #footfetishnation , #wrinkles , #thepose, #footfetish , #girlsfeet , #feet , #cute , #soles, smoothsoles, #inbed , #toes , #wringlysoles , #foottease , #freshfeet , #cutefeet, #wriglytoes , #foottease, #dirtyfeet , #feetinsandals, #feetinstockings , #FreshPaintedNails , #feetattherriver, #underwater , #toelick , #walking , #havingfun, #nocolor, #shoes , #highheels, #feetiinhighheels, #suckabletoes, #fck, #prettyfeet, #footlovers, #sexyfeet , #followme , #footgoddess , #top10toes , #teamprettyfeet , #teamprettytoes , #longtoes , #teamlongtoes , #toespread, #wooden , #sandals, #pieds, #arches, #sexysoles, #lickablefeet, #softsoles.

Make sure you fill out your Twitter bio which is a short personal description of 160 characters or fewer that is used to define who you are on Twitter.

Here are some of my favorite twitter handles:

@redpedsole[198]

@DaveKCavazos[199]

@FootFetishCandy[200]

@BarefootGirls[201]

Digital Sex Work:

YOUTUBE

It is nearly impossible to become a foot fetish goddess and launch your online empire without posting videos of your beautiful feet on Youtube.

However, Youtube seems to be coming down hard on the foot fetish community and states in their policies that you cannot upload adult content without being flagged and having your account disabled at some point. So, use caution and do blatantly use adult content words to describe your videos.

Many of the pros work around this using these vids and text as an example:

If done right, you could be one of the most popular foot fetish goddesses on the Youtube platform and send countless fans to all of your money making sites.

THE UPSELL

Make sure that you have your amateur foot fetish website URL in the description area on Youtube. What inevitably happens is that a foot lover will watch your videos, get stimulated and want to see more and possibly make a buying decision, only to find there is no link in the Youtube description box that he/she can click on and receive immediate gratification. Don't disappoint them, make sure you have your website URL easily accessible.

Just by adding a link to your Youtube description, you can upsell your custom services such as selling your worn shoes, or Niteflirt or custom photo shoot requests, etc.

Additionally, make sure that you fill out the "About" section on your Youtube channel; the more information you have to tantalize a prospect to become a repeat visitor and possible customer the better!

FLICKR

If you have a Yahoo account, you might as well go ahead and launch a Flickr account to show of your foot fetish assets. For many foot goddesses, Flickr is where they got their start before launching their full blown foot fetish empire such as *California Feet*[202] who has received over 1 million views!

Like Instagram, Flickr is one of the most popular photo sharing sites on the web and offers copyright protection from right clicking downloads of your photos. They also have a widget you can add to your website for a slide presentation effect. Check out this one from *Geisha Kia*[203].

INSTAGRAM

According to Wikipedia, Instagram is an online photo-sharing, video-sharing and social networking service that enables its users to take pictures and videos, apply digital filters to them, and share them on a variety of social networking services, such as Facebook, Twitter, Tumblr and Flickr. A distinctive feature is that it confines photos to a square shape, similar to Kodak Instamatic and Polaroid images, in contrast to the 16:9 aspect ratio now typically used by mobile device cameras. Users are also able to record and share short videos lasting for up to 15 seconds.

Instagram was created by Kevin Systrom and Mike Krieger and launched in October 2010. The service rapidly gained popularity, with over 100 million active users as of April 2012.

Instagram is a perfect platform for the amateur foot fetish model because it allows you to take photos of your feets/shoes on the go and immediately upload them to your Facebook, Twitter, Tumblr and/or Flickr account.

Instagram is an awesome way to keep your fan base engaged and expecting the unexpected; don't let them down.

PINTEREST

Pinterest[204] is a pin board-style photo-sharing website that allows users to create and manage theme-based image collections such as events, interests, and hobbies. Users can browse other pin boards for images, "re-pin" images to their own pin boards, or "like" photos. The site was founded by Ben Silbermann, Paul Sciarra and Evan

Digital Sex Work:

Sharp. It is managed by Cold Brew Labs and funded by a small group of entrepreneurs and investors.

Pinterest is the visual foot fetish lovers dream come true app because you can consume, watch and pin countless foot photos and videos until your eyes fall out!

Why Use Pinterest to Promote

There's no denying it: social media is a very powerful and influential tool for online marketing. But if you're a brand trying to build your name in the industry and want to maximize your effort, you might want to spend more time on Pinterest for the following reasons:

1. It generates a very high brand engagement.

Why is engagement important? It enhances brand recognition, helps you in assessing your marketability and promotion strategies, and strengthen your relationship with your fans. These days foot fetish fans are no longer passive. They want to make the right decisions, and they usually base theirs on what you provide them. Brand engagement is high in Pinterest, but it's not only that, more than 65 percent of it is generated by the users themselves. Simply put, they are talking about you.

2. Users are shoppers.

Despite the popularity of Facebook and Twitter, they still have to prove their capacity of generating revenues for businesses. Pinterest, on the other hand, has already shown that it can. More than 45 percent of shoppers in the United States have bought something based on recommendations they had seen on Pinterest. Best of all, they are willing to pay a lot for their orders. On the average, shoppers pay as much as $180 for each order. Conversion rate at Pinterest is currently 50 percent higher than that of the other social media and networking sites which is why Pinterest is ideal for a promoting your foot fetish site.

3. It relies heavily on visuals.

Pinterest is all about creating visual boards, and the mechanics has worked to its advantage. People, especially online foot fetish

Digital Sex Work:

shoppers, are easily drawn to images. They have a more reliable proof of the efficiency, design, and reliability of the products. Scientifically the brain processes images a lot faster than text, so we respond better and faster when we see things. Further, visual content is one of the leading, if not the main, sources of engagement.

4. It has a lot of active users.

There's a huge difference between "users" and "active users." A website can have millions of subscribers, but only few who interact with the others. Case in point is Reddit. Once in a while, it hogs the headlines because of strong opinions from its members. True enough, it has over 65 million users all around the globe, but then, surprisingly, only 2 million of a scanty 2 percent do post, comment, and use the site's features. Compare that to Pinterest, which garners 20 million active users. A huge percentage of them spends at least 15 minutes doing something, whether repinning, commenting, or liking.

5. Most of the members are mobile users.

Users share pins in their smart phones at least 3 times more often than on desktop PCs. The social media site is also beating Twitter and Facebook in iPad. Now why is the use of mobile devices essential in marketing? Experts believe that in less than 2 years, mobile devices such as smart phones and tablets will overtake desktop PCs. Mobile retail itself is showing a lot of promise. It's expected that around 15 percent of retail sales online will be fueled by the use of mobile devices.

The trick to using Pinterest for your foot fetish empire is to list as many categories as you can that are interesting and unique to your feet. For example, on my Pinterest, I list different types of feet photos/videos that "I love".

You could create a Pinterest board for a particular pair of shoes or, your soles, or red toenails, etc. Make sure you follow other foot fetish boards to begin expanding your Pinterest community as well.

Digital Sex Work:

CHAPTER 6

Interviews with Four Amateur Foot Fetish Models

Julia Lorenzi

Julia Lorenzi[205] is another Facebook friend of mine who loves showing off her high heel mules and sandals. She is Filipino and lives in Antibes; a resort town in the Alpes-Maritimes department in southeastern France. Although her feet pics are for now just a hobby for fans and admirers, at 40, she is just beginning to love her feet and more than likely turn into a full time foot Goddess.

> RedPedSole:
> How tall are you?
>
> *Julia Lorenzi:*
> *I am 1 meter and 55 inches tall.*
>
> RedPedSole:
> What do you find sexy about your feet?
>
> *Julia Lorenzi:*
> *The form of my feet and size of my feet I find sexy.*
>
> RedPedSole:
> What is your favorite nail color?
>
> *Julia Lorenzi:*
> *My favorite nail color is always red.*
>
> RedPedSole:
> How often do you get pedicures?
>
> *Julia Lorenzi:*
> *Every 15 days.*

Digital Sex Work:

RedPedSole:
What's the most expensive pair of mules you've ever worn?

Julia Lorenzi:
Its not important for me how expensive, most importantly I am very much comfortable wearing them for long hours.

RedPedSole:
Do you have photos of mules and kitten heel thongs that you can share?

Julia Lorenzi:
Yes, I have them here on my [facebook album][206] about my sexy feet.

RedPedSole:
What do you think is more sexy; high arches or wrinkled soles?

Julia Lorenzi:
More sexy to me is high arches.

RedPedSole:
When did you realize you had sexy feet?

Julia Lorenzi:
I realized having a sexy feet at the age of 40, now I love to show it!

RedPedSole:
Have you ever teased a man with your feet?

Julia Lorenzi:
Oh yes, I do love to tease a man with me with my feet a lot.

RedPedSole:
Who are some of your favorite shoe designers?

Digital Sex Work:

Julia Lorenzi:
My favorite shoe designer is <u>Gianmarco Lorenzius</u>[207]. *The best ever style of high heel shoes and boots.*

RedPedSole:
What is the most worn shoe you have in your closet that you always wear?

Julia Lorenzi:
High heel on special occasions I love to wear all the time.

RedPedSole:
Do you have a foot fetish?

Julia Lorenzi:
I never had yet a foot fetish in my life.

RedPedSole:
Do you enjoy having your feet rubbed?

Julia Lorenzi:
Oh dear yes I do love my feet rubbed feeling so sexy and could be more.

RedPedSole:
What is your favorite foot lotion?

Julia Lorenzi:
I do love Mixa Lotion. Not specifically for feet but I love it.

RedPedSole:
Have you ever had your feet worshiped, licked or kissed?

Julia Lorenzi:
Oh yes; a great experienced I've got my feet licked and sucked -- very sensual.

Digital Sex Work:

RedPedSole:
How tall of a heel do you like on your shoes?

Julia Lorenzi:
I love 6 and 7 inches tall shoes to wear.

RedPedSole:
Have men ever sent you a pair of shoes as a gift?

Julia Lorenzi:
Yes it happens. They buy shoes so sexy and I love it.

Digital Sex Work:

Latia Del Riviero

Born May 19, 1965, Vancouver, British Columbia resident, <u>Latia Del Riviero</u>[208] stands 5'2 1/2 Tall with long wavy hair and an athletic physique. She is a multi-talented dancer, choreography, martial artist and trained actress who studied at Herbert Burgoff Studios in New York City. Also a Musician and Plays Latin Percussion. But but is most known and recognized as a famous female bodybuilder who won such coveted fitness titles as the Ms. Vancouver 1987 Lightweight, Ms. Vancouver 1987 Overweight Winner, Ms. British Columbia 1987 Lightweight, Ms. British Columbia 1987 Overweight Winner, Ms. Western Canada 1989 Lightweight, Ms. Canada 1991 Lightweight, and the IFBB Professional Division Since 1991.

As one of my personal Facebook friends, I noticed Latia had a love for shoes and showing off her gorgeous feet and decided to chat with her about her perfect, petite peds.

> RedPedSole:
> When did you realize you had pretty feet?
>
> *Latia Del Riviero:*
> *I actually never did realize it, not even up to today! LOL I know one thing...They are Unique and very flexible.*
>
> RedPedSole:
> When did you notice men paying attention to your feet?
>
> *Latia Del Riviero:*
> *I noticed Men and Women liking my feet since I was 17 years old but I had a complex about having such small feet due to my family making fun of them.*
>
> RedPedSole:
> What is your favorite type of shoe(s)?
>
> *Latia Del Riviero:*
> *I love High heels, Thigh high boots, pumps and open toe shoes.*

Digital Sex Work:

RedPedSole:
When did you decide to create foot fetish videos on *Clipstore*[209]?

Latia Del Riviero:
I think I opened it two years ago, without any real expectations!

RedPedSole:
You do only softcore foot fetish videos and no nudity of any kind right?

Latia Del Riviero:
Correct! I have no nudity of any kind. All very soft core.

RedPedSole:
What is your favorite nail color?

Latia Del Riviero:
I love Red but use white a lot.

RedPedSole:
How often do you produce videos?

Latia Del Riviero:
Producing is done at least once a week or more.

RedPedSole:
Is it true that you don't like your feet?

Latia Del Riviero:
Yes, it's true that I do not like my feet because of their size. I can hardly find shoes to fit me and that is why I buy a size 6, then use insoles!

RedPedSole:
Tell me about your foot fetish and shoe group that you have on *Facebook*[210].

Digital Sex Work:

Latia Del Riviero:

I started that last year for fun, but it has taken off like crazy and the Men are so active with their positions as Admin. It was an idea that came and within seconds I created the group page! LOL

RedPedSole:

What is your favorite foot pose?

Latia Del Riviero:

My favorite foot pose? That would have to be with my toes extended as possible with my Arch at its best.

RedPedSole:

What is your favorite foot fetish video that you have done?

Latia Del Riviero:

Good question, I think I would have to go with the video of me eating grapes and banana after I peeled it!

RedPedSole:

What do you think the moral implications of having a foot fetish and being a foot fetish model has in the world?

Latia Del Riviero:

Well, what real moral implication can there really be? It's a strange fetish to those who do not have it, but if you ask me. My theory would be that any man who had a foot fetish is actually a man who loves to serve his woman. It is actually a service/worship act. My opinion only!

RedPedSole:

Do you think foot fetishism is a safe form of sexual expression?

Digital Sex Work:

Latia Del Riviero:
Absolutely! I think if the female would not see it as weird then the man would feel a whole lot more freedom to express his eroticism. That is always a great thing!

RedPedSole:
What do you think about people who say teaching women how to make money with their feet is like teaching prostitution and is a gateway to paid sex?

Latia Del Riviero:
I actually never heard of that. If someone did say it in front of me, I would call them judgmental and ignorant! SEX involves certain things... Foot Fetish is and always will be an act of Humble worship/service to me. Maybe the Men ought to be getting paid if that theory was correct about teaching women how to make money with their feet is like Prostitution! Then so would be everything else, like Massage etc. I bet the ones who agree with that have Toe jam all over their ugly feet full of bunions and stink like rotten rats!

RedPedSole:
How tall are you and what is your shoe size?

Latia Del Riviero:
I am exactly 5'1 1/4 now that I have shrunk! I was 5'2 ½. My true shoe size is 4.5-5 but wear a 6 because of my long toe nails. LOL

RedPedSole:
Do you enjoy having your feet rubbed?

Latia Del Riviero:
OMG Yes, I love my foot massages! I find it to be erotic, sensual and I am always grateful to have one! I massage my own feet all the time!

Digital Sex Work:

RedPedSole:
What is your favorite foot lotion?

Latia Del Riviero:
Any lotion that smells like flowers or almonds.

RedPedSole:
Have you ever had your feet worshiped, licked or kissed?

Latia Del Riviero:
Yes, I have had them worshiped, licked and kissed.

RedPedSole:
If so, tell us about it.

Latia Del Riviero:
It was erotic and sensual. It was relaxing and I loved every moment of it.
If I may add... It does not necessarily lead to SEX! Foot massages can alleviate pain and bring relief.

RedPedSole:
What is your favorite fragrance to put on your feet?

Latia Del Riviero:
I love pampering my feet with the best body lotion that has a seductive smell to it!

RedPedSole:
How tall of a heel do you like on your shoes?

Latia Del Riviero:
I love a minimum of 5 inches. The higher the heels, the sexier I feel!:)

Digital Sex Work:

CHECK OUT LATIA'S DIGITAL SEX WORK:

Latia's Amazon Wish List[211]

Who Am I? I Am You! by: Latia Del Riviero [Kindle Edition][212]

Panthera143 will do pics and videos of my calves, and other mild related fetishes for $5, only on fiverr.com[213]

Panthera143 will do pics and videos of my feet, and other mild fetishes for $5, only on fiverr.com[214]

Website[215]

Youtube[216]

Twitter[217]

Facebook[218]

Clipstore[219]

Digital Sex Work:

Patricia Pine of Fast Feet Meals

Patricia Pine[220] is one of my Amateur Foot Fetish clients who is now earning quite a living flexing her sexy peds around the world on the internet. She lives in New York and started with a simple Myspace page and has now expanded to several social networks.

RedPedSole:
When did your foot fetish begin?

Patricia Pine:

My foot fetish began when I was five years old in kindergarten. My teacher, Ms.Litten had some of the most sensuous pretty feet I'd ever seen. Back in that time, women were wearing Candies, which those shoes, there was a lot to see. I also like my own feet as well, and I haven't gotten over it!

RedPedSole:
What are your favorite foot poses?

Patricia Pine:

Arching my arches, by far. I was on a date a couple of years ago, and i had on black mules with black sheer hosiery. My date just keep talking and not looking my way and i was seducing a gentlemen across the way at a table. he keep noticing me, so i gave him a reason to keep staring. He actually got off, stood up, gave me this over-zealous smile and left, my date STILL didn't noticed that i was teasing him! "wink".

RedPedSole:
Why do you want to be a foot model?

Patricia Pine:

My feet are in big demand, i love teasing people with my feet, I'm also a shoe fanatic, over 200 pairs of shoes!

RedPedSole:
What is your favorite foot fetish fantasy?

Digital Sex Work:

Patricia Pine:
Have a bunch of guys worship my feet after a brutal workout.

RedPedSole:
What do you think is unique about your foot fetish site?

Patricia Pine:
Thick Chic's with hot feet! nuff fetish said!

RedPedSole:
What will visitor find at your foot fetish site?

Patricia Pine:
Its in the works!

RedPedSole:
Do you do hard core foot fetish pics/vids?

Patricia Pine:
Yes.

RedPedSole:
What are your favorite shoe to wear?

Patricia Pine:
My black flip flops, also my hooker 5 inch sandal shoes!

RedPedSole:
What is your favorite shoe to wear that makes the most noise slapping against the soles of your feet?

Patricia Pine:
My black flip flops, my main reason for wearing them! Reading my mind huh?

Digital Sex Work:

RedPedSole:
What do you what men/women to experience when they see your feet?

Patricia Pine:
For them to get horny and have their way with them.

RedPedSole:
What is your favorite foot fetish sexual position?

Patricia Pine:
On my stomach jacking off a man with my feet while he's looking at my ass.

RedPedSole:
What is your favorite nail color?

Patricia Pine:
Gold! It defines ME!!!

RedPedSole:
How often do you receive manicures/pedicures?

Patricia Pine:
Once a week, not enough? I'll let you give me a pedicure,....you probably want to! lol

RedPedSole:
Can you share one of your erotic foot fetish stories?

Patricia Pine:
This out-of-towner wanted a foot job from me. We went to a room at a motel. He was excited and nervous at the same time. I went to change into a sexy sports jersey dress, then he got REALLY excited! He took off his pants, only for me to be greeted by a delicious looking hard on!!!

Digital Sex Work:

"Calm down Girl!!!" I spent time try to shut my mouth! I oiled my feet, leaned back on my back and stroked his cock ever so slow and sensually. He was grunting and signing as this was his first ever foot job. "Oh baby, you don't know how good this shit feels!!!" his hands going through his hair, working his pelvis pushing back and forth for extra penetration. Then i stop and turned around on my back, with him looking at my ass through my white jersey dress, Long raven hair, my thick sculpted caramel thighs and my thick strong sexy feet with deep arches and wrinkles working his long thick inviting member back and forth with my feet. Within three minutes, "Damn Baby, I'm about to cum!!!" and did he ever. He came a river on me!!! It hit me fat round bum, my legs, feet, sheets and much of rug!!!! I was in such disbelief! Tempted??? lol

CHECK OUT PATRICIA'S DIGITAL SEX WORK:

MySpace 1[221]

MySpace 2[222]

Facebook[223]

Clipstore[224]

Amazon Wishlist[225]

Fetlife[226]

Sacramento Foot Factory[227]

Digital Sex Work:

California Feet

California Feet is a full time Med student living in San Francisco. She has the most beautiful feet and flawless skin tone you have ever seen and is fast becoming an internet sensation and success story with over 1 million views on her [Flickr account](228)! Born August 9th, she says, "*I have a foot fetish, not only for my feet but for other peoples feet, I can appreciate a gorgeous foot regardless of gender.*"

>RedPedSole:
>What is your ethnicity?
>
>*California Feet:*
>*I am black, Mexican and Puerto Rican.*
>
>RedPedSole:
>How old are you?
>
>*California Feet:*
>*I am 26 years old.*
>
>RedPedSole:
>How tall are you?
>
>*California Feet:*
>*I am 5'4.*
>
>RedPedSole:
>What is the tattoo on your right thigh?
>
>*California Feet:*
>*I have an anatomically correct heart on my right thigh; it's a tattoo I got with my best friend because she and I are both lovers of the human body.*
>
>RedPedSole:
>When did you realize you had pretty feet?

Digital Sex Work:

California Feet:

I was in high school when I began to admire my feet in the way that I do now.

RedPedSole:

When did you notice men liking and wanting your feet?

California Feet:

I was 17 when I encountered a young man that admired feet and he was the first person to suck my toes.

RedPedSole:

Why did you choose the name "California Feet"?

California Feet:

I was making a youtube account to link some of videos to flickr and I was thinking of screen names that I have and I have one named "kalifornien sonnenuntergang" which means California sunset in German and I wanted something similar but in English and I came up with "californiafeet" since I live in California and it was youtube for my feet. Ever since then it just stuck.

RedPedSole:

When did you first have foot sex and how did it feel?

California Feet:

I had foot sex for the first time when I was 23 years old with my very first footman and it was awesome! I love giving foot jobs and I absolutely love feeling the warm aftermath in-between my toes and such.

RedPedSole:

You have the most beautiful soles on the Internet; how do you take care of your feet?

Digital Sex Work:

California Feet:

Thank you! I use a great callus eliminator that is very effective; I also use a bleaching cream on any scars I might obtain from wearing new sandals and such.

RedPedSole:

Dumb, question...why do you like having your feet licked and sucked?

California Feet:

Definitely not a dumb question but my reasoning for liking it is because it feels great! It does something to my loins and I feel very dominant in the situation.

RedPedSole:

Do you have an Amazon wishlist? If so, why?

California Feet:

I do have an Amazon wishlist and the reason why I have one is because I encountered a female fetishist that had one and I thought it was super cool that people could buy "you" things for posting photos or videos.

RedPedSole:

Do you sell old, worn flip flops, shoes, stockings?

California Feet:

I have been known to sell old shoes, socks and flip-flops.

RedPedSole:

Where else on the web do you promote your foot fetish?

California Feet:

I am on flickr, facebook, twitter, youtube, fetlife, and instagram.

Digital Sex Work:

RedPedSole:
What's the most outrageous amount of money have you made using your feet?

California Feet:
50 dollars for a ten minute webcam session seemed outrageous but someone paid it willingly on a few occasions, in addition to 3 hundred dollars for a few hours of my time.

RedPedSole:
What's the craziest request you've ever gotten about your feet?

California Feet:
Stepping on a little animal, I of course declined the request as it was against my morals.

RedPedSole:
How do you set up your lights; if at all?

California Feet:
I currently do not have a light setup but it is something I am looking into.

RedPedSole:
You told me your boyfriend isn't into feet like your fans; explain?

California Feet:
That is correct, my partner has come to learn to appreciate a gorgeous, well taken care of foot but he isn't compelled to suck my toes or lick my soles.

RedPedSole:
Tell me about the services you provide with your feet.

Digital Sex Work:

California Feet:
I provide webcam shows with my feet, personalized videos and photos, used footwear.

RedPedSole:
You engage in both soft core and hard-core sessions; how does your boyfriend feel about his girl giving another guy a footjob?

California Feet:
My partner doesn't mind me doing the foot thing as long as I'm safe and I don't engage in sexual intercourse with my foot guy. When I would come home post foot session he would look at my feet and then he'd jokingly say "Can I touch them?" and laugh. I would then walk to the bathroom and wash my feet and sandals with antibacterial soap in the bathtub.

RedPedSole:
Is it true that he doesn't like sucking your toes?

California Feet:
My partner isn't a fan of toe sucking or sole licking but he has voiced an interest in rubbing lotion on his female friends feet, which I welcome.

RedPedSole:
Describe your first paid footjob session.

California Feet:
My first paid footjob session was nerve wracking at first, as I was meeting someone I hadn't met in real life prior to that night but I warmed up to him quickly. He then massaged my feet and by far the best massage I have ever had to this date, he then got on his knees and sucked my toes, licked my soles and then I gave him a footjob. It was pretty awesome after that and I saw him a few times a month for 8 months or so.

Digital Sex Work:

RedPedSole:
How do ensure your safety?

California Feet:
I don't meet every person that wants to worship my feet but I usually pick men that have children, or very professional jobs and that way I feel like they have something to lose and they won't try anything stupid.

RedPedSole:
Do you ever go beyond foot worship?

California Feet:
Do you ever show more than your feet in paid sessions? I do not go beyond foot worship out of respect for my partner and for the fact that they (the foot friend) would always expect more every session.

RedPedSole:
How have you managed not getting banned by YouTube?

California Feet:
I try to keep my videos PG and not talk about having my toes sucked and fucked.

RedPedSole:
You say even your Grandmother knows about your FF business and is cool with it?

California Feet:
My grandma is indeed aware of my foot doings and she often gives me tips on how to make more money. It's pretty funny. lol

RedPedSole:
Is there a part of your personality where you like men to be submissive to you?

Digital Sex Work:

California Feet:

Or do you get a sense of pleasure pleasing a man with your feet? It goes both ways, I love being very dominant in a way and I look ordering my foot friend to do specific things to my feet and beg to have them (my feet/toes) in their lap, and mouth and so on. I also like a man that takes charge and tells me what he wants and what he likes it's very sexy.

RedPedSole:

How do you come up with your nail designs?

California Feet:

I follow nail art blogs and nail polish websites.

RedPedSole:

A hot new trend on Youtube is JOE, "Jerk Off Encouragement" or JOI, Jerk Off Instruction. How popular has this type of video been for you?

California Feet:

I have only made one which was available on my friends Clips4Sale website and it sold quite a few copies. I refuse to post one on YouTube, as I don't want someone underage to encounter it and that is the reason why I don't talk about my feet in a sexual way on YouTube.

RedPedSole:

How do you feel about the moral and ethics of being a foot goddess and having men pay to play with your feet?

California Feet:

I find it to be difficult as my moral compass might be a bit different than most foot girls; I find it hard (for myself) to ask for things or to take insane amounts of money for doing very little. However, my college student self talks me into taking some of the offers, as my textbooks can be pretty costly.

Digital Sex Work:

RedPedSole:

How do you think society in general views the FF lifestyle from a moral and ethical perspective?

California Feet:

From personal experience I know quite a few people who think feet and foot fetishes are absolutely disgusting and that seems to pretty much the "norm" for a lot of the people that I encounter.

RedPedSole:

How old were you when you realized that you had pretty feet and you liked looking at both men and womens feet?

California Feet:

I would say I was about 15 when I realized that I had "pretty" feet and I have always noticed feet (male and female) ever since I was a child.

RedPedSole:

How much does it cost in nail polish and foot care a month to maintain your perfect feet?

California Feet:

I use somewhat expensive nail polish that costs $8-$10 per bottle but I don't buy it every month. I would say it's relatively inexpensive to do my weekly pedicures if I really calculated the cost. I would say less than $20 per month (if I don't buy new polish) since I do everything myself.

RedPedSole:

So, you are using your FF business to pay for college? I understand you would like to be a cardiologist someday?

California Feet:

I currently have a scholarship so I don't use my FF activities to pay for college but it is a nice source of supplemental income.

Digital Sex Work:

RedPedSole:
Do you have women who hate on you because you have so many admirers and fans from around the world?

California Feet:
I have not encountered a female of that nature but I am sure there are a few, as there always is.

RedPedSole:
What are some of your other hobbies not related to FF; such as movies, wine tasting, etc?

California Feet:
I enjoy doing outdoorsy things, such as camping, hiking, going to the beach, I love riding my longboard skateboard, bowling, drinking socially with friend and family, researching science, and reading medical journals.

RedPedSole:
What is your ultimate goal as a foot goddess?

California Feet:
I never really thought about it like that and I never anticipated that I would have so many foot friends that enjoy looking at my feet as much as I do. I guess I could only hope for is to open peoples eyes to foot fetish if they have not been exposed to it before. My best friend hated feet for such a long time but recently she has expressed her admiration for her own feet and it made me happy to hear her say that.

RedPedSole:
What advice would you give amateur foot model wanting to launch their own foot fetish YouTube or website?

California Feet:
I would tell an amateur foot model that they don't have to put up with pushy "fans" if they don't want to, don't let people take

Digital Sex Work:

advantage of you, to charge people for requests, and don't sell out your soul (sole) for a little bit of money! Stay true to yourself.

Interesting Fun Facts About California Feet:

- I find the smell of food nauseating

- I'm a nice girl until someone pisses me off (pretty hard to do) and then I turn into a stereotypical black girl.

- When I talk to my best friend I talk like "Tony Montana" from scarface.

- I have only dated 3 dudes in my lifetime and they have all been white dudes.

- I'm the youngest of 5 children, my siblings are 40, 38, 36, and 34 years old.

- I think older men are so friggin sexy!!

- I love watching men shave.

- Sometimes when I see absolutely gorgeous feet I wish I had a dick so I could fuxk them. Lol

- I paint my own toenails because I'm too embarrassed for the nail tech's to see them without polish.

- I have never had my toes sucked whilst engaging in intercourse and I probably will never experience it. (Not taking any offers) lol

- I do ballerina arch stretches to obtain a higher arch. It works!

- My best friend "J" and I quote movies like "belly", "scarface", and "a Bronx tale" when we talk to each other. We also talk in code when were around other people.

- After I lost my virginity I didn't have sex again until 17 months later.

- I found my soulmate, he's a 34 year old physician who now lives in Michigan.

- I have a super corny sense of humor. I always make pun-nies. Lol

- I only wear Victoria Secret under garments.

Digital Sex Work:

CHECK OUT CALIFORNIA'S DIGITAL SEX WORK:

Flickr[229]

Calfifornia Feet's Amazon Wishlist[230]

Facebook[231]

Youtube[232]

Fetlife[233]

#

Digital Sex Work:

RESOURCES & RECOMMENDATIONS

Recommended Viewing

<u>Hot Legs Workout Guide: "Insanely Simple and Quick Workout Program That Anyone Can Use to Get Heavenly Legs. 4 Weeks Program Used By National Body Champion Ensures Results!"</u>[234]

<u>Iphone Photography Magic - Trick Photography With Your Iphone - "Discover the Simple Secrets To Taking Jaw-Dropping Pictures On Your Camera Phone And Receiving Thousands of Views and Likes on Photo sharing Websites!"</u>[235]

Recommended Surfing

<u>http://www.pinterest.com/TheRedPedSole</u>[236]

<u>http://sacramentofootfactory.wordpress.com/</u>[237]

<u>https://twitter.com/redpedsole</u>[238]

<u>http://www.youtube.com/redpedsole</u>[239]

<u>https://fetlife.com/users/1048091</u>[240]

<u>https://www.youtube.com/channel/UC1WXKoGYvka-LXu_nMmnP7w</u>[241]

ABOUT THE AUTHOR

RedPedSole is a veteran Internet Marketer, SEO and Social Media Marketing Specialist who adores female feet.

My Pen Name is RedPedSole; I am a seasoned internet marketer, SEO and social media marketing specialist. I enjoy the foot fetish lifestyle and I really enjoy teaching women how to reinvent their lives and earn substantial money using their most beautiful asset; their feet!

I work with women exclusively and am particularly fond of BBW's of all ethnicities. I enjoy writing "How to" books and also host a popular internet radio, tv and blog show.

Digital Sex Work:

ACKNOWLEDGMENTS

Special Thanks to:

Latia Del Riviero

Julia Lorenzi

Patricia Pine

Angela Starks

Cindy Ray

Rainha Grazi

Kat Kidwell

Tony Moreno

Dr. Yvonne Fulbright

Thank you for downloading Digital Sex Work! Please fill out your e-mail address to receive our Digital Sex Work eCourse and Updates!

Digital Sex Work:

INDEX

Bonus Content

[1] *8-Day eCourse, Newsletter and Updates*
http://ymlp.com/xgbhuuwygmgj

[2] *Sex Work*
http://en.wikipedia.org/wiki/Sex_work

[3] *Erotic Crone*
https://fetlife.com/users/1034117

[4] *Is Sex Work Becoming 'No Big Deal'?*
http://huff.to/1dZ8ccp

[5] *Nouse, York*
http://bit.ly/H1m0oH

[6] *Philippe Matthews*
http://www.thepmshow.tv/

Preface

[7] *Philippe Matthews Show blog*
http://thepmshow.tv/channel/love-relationships/the-popularity-of-50-shades-of-grey/

[8] *worship women*
http://bit.ly/11SLMkV

[9] *WATN-TV Local 24 News*
http://bit.ly/16lv6bC

[10] *Homeless Man With Foot Fetish Plead No Contest To Charges*
http://cbsloc.al/17YYfn8

[11] *Sacramento News & Review*
http://bit.ly/17Z05EF

[12] *here*
http://www.sacda.org/assets/pdf/pr/cases_interest/COI_William%20Russell.pdf

Digital Sex Work:

[13] *TMZ*
http://youtu.be/FVq7zR4MR_Y

[14] *Adult Entertainment Expo*
http://tmz.me/17DgCic

[15] *Rex Ryan Foot Video*
http://www.tmz.com/videos/0_6k2hg5gf/

[16] *Christian Louboutins*
http://dailym.ai/1eD06Uu

[17] *The Quentin Tarantino Toe-Sucking Sex Email That Will Haunt Your Dreams*
http://bit.ly/17aOoRM

[18] *Quentin Tarantino Talks Feet, Fear & Films*
http://bit.ly/1cLPOAY

[19] *Quinton Tarantino's Foot Fetish*
https://www.facebook.com/pages/Quentin-Tarantinos-Foot-Fetish/242004779177025

[20] *Quentin Tarantino's Foot Fetish*
http://bit.ly/H5xtEf

[21] *Quentin Tarantino Spoof Compilation and Foot Scenes on YouTube*
http://bit.ly/1gYSgXy

[22] *Ask.fm*
http://bit.ly/1hk2amI

[23] *Celebrity Foot Fetish*
http://voices.yahoo.com/celebrity-foot-fetish-foot-fetish-which-321765.html

[24] *IMDb*
http://imdb.to/16Qnagu

[25] *Foot fetishism*
http://en.wikipedia.org/wiki/Foot_fetishism

[26] *Official Website*
http://www.sexualitysource.com/

[27] *Twitter*
https://twitter.com/YvonneFulbright

Digital Sex Work:

Chapter 1

[28] *Treat Your Feet: Exercises To Treat And Prevent Common Foot Ailments*
http://7d0f6pnkr82g6tc3re2zlj1hbu.hop.clickbank.net/

[29] *CureMySweatyFeet.com*
http://66202dnlk9uefs110q4jxzhc5o.hop.clickbank.net/

[30] *toe rings*
http://bit.ly/1b2CvMp

[31] *bold nail colors*
http://bit.ly/HbqeKu

[32] *Facebook*
https://www.facebook.com/fernanda.amarante.37

[33] *Sacramentofootfactory's Blog*
http://bit.ly/16DE8Rq

[34] *Cindy Ray's*
http://bit.ly/1g6oyAZ

[35] *Instagram*
http://instagram.com/p/gARtzxCP3J/

[36] *Website 1*
http://www.arch-angeluk.com/

[37] *Website 2*
http://www.mistresscindyray.com/

[38] *Clipstore*
http://clips4sale.com/store/19535

[39] *Email*
http://bit.ly/1io4arI

[40] *, Rainha Grazi*
http://bit.ly/1io4arI

[41] *website*
http://www.goddessgrazi.com/

[42] *Twitter*
https://twitter.com/goddessgrazi

Digital Sex Work:

[43] *Facebook*
https://www.facebook.com/pages/Goddess-Grazi/373397596028102

[44] *Youtube*
http://www.youtube.com/user/GoddessGrazi

[45] *Flickr*
http://www.flickr.com/photos/goddessgrazi/

[46] *Blogspot*
http://goddessgrazi.blogspot.com.br/

[47] *Instagram*
http://instagram.com/goddessgrazi

[48] *toe rings*
https://www.facebook.com/ToeRingsPage

[49] *Britney Spears*
http://www.huffingtonpost.com/2012/07/18/kim-kardashian-britney-spears-toe-rings_n_1677988.html

[50] *ToeRings.com*
http://www.toerings.com/

[51] *barefoot sandals*
https://www.facebook.com/FFJdesigns

[52] *foot worship*
https://www.facebook.com/pages/Foot-worship-Fétichisme-du-pied-Tunisia/392150767547112

[53] *dirty feet*
https://www.facebook.com/groups/2384305501/

[54] *soles*
http://www.pinterest.com/pedsole/soles-i-love/

[55] *mules*
http://www.pinterest.com/pedsole/mules-i-love/

[56] *flip flops*
https://www.facebook.com/groups/440146476048443/

[57] *self toe sucking*
https://www.facebook.com/groups/139400199519574/

Digital Sex Work:

[58] *toe licking*
https://www.facebook.com/pages/Toe-sucking/106572159380170

[59] *BBW (Big Beautiful Women)*
https://www.facebook.com/BBWfeet

[60] *pantyhose & stocking feet*
https://www.facebook.com/groups/Nylon.Feet.Fetish/

[61] *celebrity feet*
https://www.facebook.com/pages/Celebrity-Feet/346937578670754

[62] *pedicure feet*
https://www.facebook.com/groups/300895493366240/

[63] *painted toes*
https://www.facebook.com/pages/Painted-toes/335126296582972

[64] *sexy shoes*
https://www.facebook.com/SexyShoess

[65] *toes & soles*
https://www.facebook.com/pages/Sexy-Soles-and-Toes/280096638771181

[66] *Asian women's cute sexy feet*
https://www.facebook.com/SweetAsianFeetAndTickling

[67] *Asian Fetish*
http://en.wikipedia.org/wiki/Asian_fetish

[68] *Asian women's feet*
http://youtu.be/YI4_-Qd4u_A

[69] *Henna*
http://sacramentofootfactory.wordpress.com/2013/10/16/the-beauty-of-henna-feet/

[70] *variety of designs*
https://www.facebook.com/pages/CUTE-Indian-FEET/286497608147448

[71] *Henna foot designs*
https://www.facebook.com/pages/Goddess-Feet-Collection/504858742899781

[72] *henna foot tattoos*
http://www.pinterest.com/pedsole/henna-designs-i-love/

Digital Sex Work:

[73] *Ebony Feet*
https://www.facebook.com/groups/prettyblackwomenfeet/

[74] *Italian Feet*
https://www.facebook.com/SexyItalianFeet

[75] *Latina Feet*
https://www.facebook.com/pages/Sweet-Latina-Feet/121160921361592

[76] *Lebanese Feet*
https://www.facebook.com/groups/159530984097944/

[77] *Miss America*
http://en.wikipedia.org/wiki/Vanessa_L._Williams

[78] *feet with face*
http://www.ducksfeetlinks.com/category/feet-without-face-1.html

[79] *feet with face*
http://bit.ly/1gpK3Nq

[80] *Sacramento Foot Fetish Factory*
https://sacramentofootfactory.wordpress.com/

[81] *Geisha Kia*
http://loveliestfeet.blogspot.com/

[82] *Tiffany's Tumblr*
http://footsietiffany.tumblr.com/

[83] *Wordpress.org*
http://www.wordpress.org/

[84] *BlueHost.com*
http://www.bluehost.com/track/mime

[85] *HostGator*
http://secure.hostgator.com/~affiliat/cgi-bin/affiliates/clickthru.cgi?id=revshock

[86] *cpanel overview*
https://www.youtube.com/watch?v=Hyp-BcFqkfw

[87] *Wordpress Cpanel Install*
http://bit.ly/WUD7LB

[88] *Using cPanel with WordPress Website Hosting*
http://bit.ly/YDWpnM

[89] *How to Set Up a Hosted WordPress Site*
http://on.mash.to/1aD7W1K

Chapter 2

[90] *Victoria Secret Blush*
http://www.amazon.com/gp/product/B007SNFKBG/ref=as_li_tf_tl?ie=UTF8&camp=1789&creative=9325&creativeASIN=B007SNFKBG&linkCode=as2&tag=shockpublishi-20

[91] *Facebook*
https://www.facebook.com/pages/Kitty-Kat-Closet/117026651779948

[92] *Pinterest*
http://www.pinterest.com/Kittykatcloset/

[93] *Twitter*
https://twitter.com/KittyKatCloset

[94] *Friedman's Etsy Shop*
http://www.etsy.com/people/MoniqueFriedman

[95] *Pinterest*
http://www.pinterest.com/flipinista/

[96] *Twitter*
https://twitter.com/Flipinista

[97] *The Soles of Scarlett Maria Ujueta*
http://bit.ly/1eYwxgq

[98] *Vietnam Soles*
http://youtu.be/A7aBLgnr3as

[99] *Colorful Toes*
http://bit.ly/1caKK8g

[100] *Scarlett Maria Ujueta's Colorful Toes*
http://bit.ly/1hlVMLT

[101] *Blue Pantyhose*
http://on.fb.me/17SMAZ2

Digital Sex Work:

[102] *Great Pantyhose Business Meeting*
http://www.youtube.com/watch?v=qacFGNfeWhg

[103] *Fishnets and Pink Polish*
http://youtu.be/Du3R5ekY2aY

[104] *1 Dollar Thongs To Black Patent Slides*
http://bit.ly/12epI3x

[105] *Golden Mules 1*
http://bit.ly/11jGm30

[106] *Pedal Pump*
http://bit.ly/14Md3t6

[107] *Sexy Mules*
http://youtu.be/N7YjTo3p6ck

[108] *Thong sandals flip flop*
http://bit.ly/YRBXDt

[109] *HD Feet Heaven*
http://youtu.be/atlKBBbf93U

[110] *Glasses Crush2*
http://youtube/G5Z1Y6KJ4C8

[111] *Pedal Pumping*
http://bit.ly/1bXa7tB

[112] *Thong Sandals with Nice Pedi*
http://youtu.be/PIIgmKm4Isg

[113] *Sexy Feet Dangling in White Mules*
http://bit.ly/1aNY6Vk

[114] *Flip Flops Dangling*
http://youtu.be/TKRsAJ4gyT4

[115] *Sacramento Foot Factory*
http://bit.ly/11anLnN

[116] *Meet Kia & Her Feet*
http://youtu.be/ErOFqJ-P6Wk

[117] *foot fetish videos*
http://bit.ly/12cSyVH

[118] *fiverr.com*
http://bit.ly/15fWcRm

[119] *Clips4sale*
http://clips4sale.com/31742/7995429

[120] *Sexy Feet JOE*
http://youtu.be/VunLvzUPxqE

[121] *My Day On Mules*
http://www.youtube.com/watch?v=ptbwVQH2Gs4

[122] *Walking in High Heel Mules*
http://youtu.be/vfhYC5uoTWI

[123] *Wooden Exercises*
http://youtu.be/AANmeHu37Yo

[124] *Another Sweet Pair of High Heel Mules*
http://youtu.be/lSJ4BioJmOc

Chapter 3

[125] *amazon*
http://amzn.to/11kXwuX

[126] *Happy Wednesday*
http://youtu.be/TsCtK5oxgB8

Chapter 4

[127] *Isabelle Shy selling her Colin Stuart sandals*
http://www.youtube.com/watch?v=lNv_2maqmFk&feature=share&list=UUm2HnXjNrlroLfyeR5pTHug

[128] *worn shoes*
http://bit.ly/13kioEf

[129] *Women's Shoes For Sale*
https://fetlife.com/groups/23090

Digital Sex Work:

[130] *Facebook*
https://fetlife.com/groups/23090

[131] *http://www.shockshoppingcart.com*
http://www.shockshoppingcart.com

[132] *The Foot Geisha*
http://clips4sale.com/store/47531

[133] *Muscle Goddess, Latia Del Riviero*
http://bit.ly/Z62ZtI

[134] *Camilafootmodel*
http://www.images4sale.com/store/71306

[135] *Feet Jeans*
http://bit.ly/15eTdrH

[136] *DesignerShoes.com*
http://www.shareasale.com/r.cfm?b=411247&u=505291&m=16931&urllink=&aftrack=

[137] *Feet Factor*
http://www.feetfactory.com/tour/track/2352383

[138] *I Love Long Toes*
http://www.ilovelongtoes.com/tour/track/2352383/

[139] *LongToes.com*
http://www.longtoes.com/tour/track/2352383/

[140] *Official Fifty Shades of Grey Sex Toys*
http://www.gopjn.com/t/R0JGRUVMTUtCRkVNSkdMQk1LSUtM

[141] *smart shopping cart*
http://www.shockshoppingcart.com

[142] *Panthera143 will pics and videos of my feet, and other mild fetishes for $5, only on fiverr.com*
http://bit.ly/15fWcRm

[143] *Panthera143 will videos of my feet, and other mild related fetishes for $5, only on fiverr.com*
http://bit.ly/147u90d

Digital Sex Work:

[144] *Shineykisses will write anything anywhere on my feet for you for $5, only on fiverr.com*
http://bit.ly/12P2UJr

[145] *Shineykisses will take a video of my feet for $5, only on fiverr.com*
http://bit.ly/UarCyY

[146] *Brookevelyn will take pictures of my feet in any way you wish in less than 24 hours for $5, only on fiverr.com*
http://bit.ly/10y8TCJ

[147] *Deadlittlebunny will paint my toes the color of your choice and send you a picture for $5, only on fiverr.com*
http://bit.ly/VbGqN7

[148] *Blackbootiegirl will make a 30 second video clip with your name on a sticker and place it between my ebony soles for $5, only on fiverr.com*
http://bit.ly/TQsNXT

[149] *Bikinigirl will take a picture of my feet with heels or not for $5, only on fiverr.com*
http://bit.ly/RnHBLl

[150] *Hcpinterns will send you a sexy video tease in black pantyhose nylons for $5, only on fiverr.com*
http://bit.ly/ZKySrk

[151] *global search*
http://bit.ly/RYMDzt

[152] *Paypal*
https://www.paypal.com/us/mrb/pal=5ZGWRTT636LSY

[153] *Dwolla*
https://www.dwolla.com/

[154] *http://www.fiverr.com*
http://www.fiverr.com/

[155] *Amazon.com Wish-list*
http://amzn.to/109HIgk

[156] *store info*
http://www.clips4sale.com/do/storeinfo

Digital Sex Work:

[157] *Camila Mercedes De Bellucci*
http://bit.ly/Hbxhmk

[158] *Clips4sale*
http://www.clips4sale.com/71306

[159] *Camilafootmodel*
https://www.facebook.com/Camilafootmodel

[160] *Twitter*
https://twitter.com/CamilaFootmodel

[161] *imgChili*
http://imgchili.com/

[162] *FAQ*
http://imgchili.com/faq

[163] *demo*
http://imgchili.com/album/01a2a27b22d5374998caf8add768d1f9

[164] *link*
http://imgchili.com/show/2077/2077195_2011_08_19_2337.png

[165] *Adult Only*
http://bit.ly/12IupEz

[166] *HiddenAuctions.com*
http://bit.ly/139ehcW

[167] *Niteflirt*
http://bit.ly/10dG6xW

[168] *Niteflirt business*
http://bit.ly/11ElnWN

[169] *ElegantBareFeet.com*
http://elegantbarefeet.com/

[170] *Aweber*
http://www.aweber.com/

[171] *YourMailingListProvider*
http://ymlp.com/

[172] *Ebanned.net*
http://ebanned.net/

[173] *AdultWork.com*
http://www.adultwork.com

Chapter 5

[174] *Fetlife.com*
http://www.fetlife.com

[175] *Fetlife Ads*
https://fetlife.com/ads

[176] *Patrica Pine*
http://on.fb.me/11Engms

[177] *The Sole Lounge*
http://on.fb.me/16isU2d

[178] *Red Ped Sole*
https://www.facebook.com/redpedsole

[179] *We Love Womens Feet*
https://www.facebook.com/WeLoveWomensFeet

[180] *My Feet Fetish*
https://www.facebook.com/my.feet.fetish

[181] *Feet Lovers Tunisia*
https://www.facebook.com/pages/Feet-lovers-tunisia/483590571686133

[182] *I Love Feet Nails*
https://www.facebook.com/ILoveFeetNails?ref=ts&fref=ts

[183] *Natasha Lov Feett*
https://www.facebook.com/natasha.lov.14?ref=ts&fref=ts

[184] *Lynn Jones*
https://www.facebook.com/lynn.jones.39395033

[185] *Foot Fetish Videos*
https://www.facebook.com/pages/Foot-FetisH-Videos/170585679748280

[186] *Cayenne Soles*
https://www.facebook.com/CayenneSoles

Digital Sex Work:

[187] *Natasha Lov Feet*
https://www.facebook.com/NatashaLovFeet

[188] *Feet Licking*
https://www.facebook.com/pages/Feet-Licking/328784037217376

[189] *Feetwin.com*
http://bit.ly/1bUGrl1

[190] *ToeBunny*
http://feetwin.com/user/Toebunny

[191] *joined immediately*
http://feetwin.com/user/redpedsole

[192] *blogging platform*
http://feetwin.com/blogs

[193] *Tumblr.com*
http://www.tumblr.com/

[194] *How To*
http://www.youtube.com/watch?v=Ciqflh8VsdQ

[195] *Tiffany*
http://footsietiffany.tumblr.com/

[196] *Hashtags*
http://bit.ly/155ktnu

[197] *Wikipedia*
http://en.wikipedia.org/wiki/Hashtag

[198] *@redpedsole*
http://www.twitter.com/redpedsole

[199] *@DaveKCavazos*
http://www.twitter.com/DaveKCavazos

[200] *@FootFetishCandy*
http://www.twitter.com/FootFetishCandy

[201] *@BarefootGirls*
http://www.twitter.com/BarefootGirls

[202] *California Feet*
http://www.flickr.com/photos/hellagnarly/

Digital Sex Work:

[203] *Geisha Kia*
http://bit.ly/ZllJmZ

[204] *Pinterest*
http://www.pinterest.com/pedsole/

Chapter 6

[205] *Julia Lorenzi*
https://www.facebook.com/julia.lorenzi.3?fref=ts

[206] *facebook album*
https://www.facebook.com/julia.lorenzi.3/media_set?set=a.10200576833696261.1073741828.1621613412&type=3

[207] *Gianmarco Lorenzius*
http://www.gianmarcolorenzius.com/

[208] *Latia Del Riviero*
https://www.facebook.com/groups/SexyShoesandFeet

[209] *Clipstore*
http://clips4sale.com/studio/42900/9741929/cidNS4xLjIuMy43Ni4wLjAuMC4w

[210] *Facebook*
https://www.facebook.com/groups/SexyShoesandFeet

[211] *Latia's Amazon Wish List*
http://www.amazon.com/gp/registry/wishlist/1G0WFDZIP4513

[212] *Who Am I? I Am You! by: Latia Del Riviero [Kindle Edition]*
http://bit.ly/17O1JQ0

[213] *Panthera143 will do pics and videos of my calves, and other mild related fetishes for $5, only on fiverr.com*
http://bit.ly/147u90d

[214] *Panthera143 will do pics and videos of my feet, and other mild fetishes for $5, only on fiverr.com*
http://bit.ly/15fWcRm

[215] *Website*
http://www.latiadelriviero.com/

Digital Sex Work:

[216] *Youtube*
http://www.youtube.com/user/latiadelriviero

[217] *Twitter*
https://twitter.com/latiadelriviero

[218] *Facebook*
https://www.facebook.com/latiadelriviero

[219] *Clipstore*
http://clips4sale.com/studio/42900/9741929/cidNS4xLjIuMy43Ni4wLjAuMC4w

[220] *Patricia Pine*
http://fastfeetmeals.com/

[221] *MySpace 1*
http://www.myspace.com/primetimejody

[222] *MySpace 2*
https://myspace.com/keychameleon

[223] *Facebook*
https://www.facebook.com/patrica.pine.3

[224] *Clipstore*
http://www.clips4sale.com/54493

[225] *Amazon Wishlist*
https://www.amazon.com/gp/gift-central/organizer?ie=UTF8&id=XKUGOXN3BB2F&ref_=cm_go_nav_recip_pp

[226] *Fetlife*
https://fetlife.com/users/1049851

[227] *Sacramento Foot Factory*
http://sacramentofootfactory.wordpress.com/?s=janna

[228] *Flickr account!*
http://www.flickr.com/photos/hellagnarly/

[229] *Flickr*
http://www.flickr.com/photos/hellagnarly/

[230] *Calfifornia Feet's Amazon Wishlist*
http://amzn.com/w/1IBEUH7Q3JTSB

Digital Sex Work:

[231] *Facebook*
http://facebook.com/Californiafeet

[232] *Youtube*
http://www.youtube.com/user/californiafeet

[233] *Fetlife*
https://fetlife.com/users/1894753

Resources & Recommendations

[234] *Hot Legs Workout Guide: "Insanely Simple and Quick Workout Program That Anyone Can Use to Get Heavenly Legs. 4 Weeks Program Used By National Body Champion Ensures Results!*
http://cafb7mlekh-7du3-rzu95r8n9x.hop.clickbank.net/

[235] *Iphone Photography Magic - Trick Photography With Your Iphone - "Discover the Simple Secrets To Taking Jaw-Dropping Pictures On Your Camera Phone And Receiving Thousands of Views and Likes on Photo sharing Websites!*
http://449afjjcoczfcpcbmgs7r8qj3v.hop.clickbank.net

[236] *http://www.pinterest.com/TheRedPedSole*
http://www.pinterest.com/TheRedPedSole

[237] *http://sacramentofootfactory.wordpress.com*
http://sacramentofootfactory.wordpress.com/

[238] *https://twitter.com/redpedsole*
https://twitter.com/redpedsole

[239] *http://www.youtube.com/redpedsole*
http://www.youtube.com/redpedsole

[240] *https://fetlife.com/users/1048091*
https://fetlife.com/users/1048091

[241] *https://www.youtube.com/channel/UC1WXKoGYvka-LXu_nMmnP7w*
https://www.youtube.com/channel/UC1WXKoGYvka-LXu_nMmnP7w

www.ingramcontent.com/pod-product-compliance
Lightning Source LLC
Chambersburg PA
CBHW051722170526
45167CB00002B/763